Applying Family Therapy

A Guide for Caring Professionals in the Community

Steven Walker
and
Jane Akister

Russell House Publishing

First published in 2004 by:
Russell House Publishing Ltd.
4 St. George's House
Uplyme Road
Lyme Regis
Dorset DT7 3LS

Tel: 01297-443948
Fax: 01297-442722
e-mail: help@russellhouse.co.uk
www.russellhouse.co.uk

British Library Cataloguing-in-publication Data:
A catalogue record for this book is available from the British Library.

ISBN: 1-903855-40-3

Typeset by TW Typesetting, Plymouth, Devon

Printed by Antony Rowe, Chippenham

About Russell House Publishing

RHP is a group of social work, probation, education and youth and community work practitioners and academics working in collaboration with a professional publishing team.

Our aim is to work closely with the field to produce innovative and valuable materials to help managers, trainers, practitioners and students.

We are keen to receive feedback on publications and new ideas for future projects. For details of our other publications please visit our website or ask us for a catalogue. Contact details are on this page.

Contents

Dedication

To our families

Preface

There are but two families in the world as my grandmother used to say, the Haves and the Have-nots.

(Cervantes)

Practitioners and other professionals encounter families in almost every aspect of their practice in whatever context and with whatever service user group. The family is the focus of health and social policy strategy across a range of central and local government and health service provision, including criminal justice, mental health, community care, youth offending, fostering and adoption, education and primary health care. Families are often stated to be at the heart of government policies that aim to support parents and children to participate equally in society as valued citizens. The recent government policy initiative on child welfare *Every Child Matters* (DfES, 2003) the new Children Act and the Children's NSF herald structural changes in the delivery of children's services into Children's Trusts that will require highly skilled competent practitioners with the skills provided by a family therapy approach. The increasing trend towards multi-disciplinary team working requires practitioners to identify and distinguish the knowledge, values and methods they can bring to bear in such contexts. Family therapy as a form of intervention, and the systems theory underpinning it, offer an attractive, accessible and flexible approach to practice in a variety of agency contexts.

Family therapy has changed considerably since it first emerged during the 1950s as an alternative to individual psychodynamic practice. It has moved beyond the narrow clinical setting dominated by psychiatrists and psychologists to be enthusiastically taken up by nurses, support staff, practitioners and voluntary agency staff in their community-based contexts. From a model of practice with a narrow range of techniques and theoretical assumptions, family therapy has broadened its intellectual repertoire to embrace new developments in social constructionism, narrative therapy and post-modern concepts. It is undoubtedly better informed by feminist, service-user and anti-racist ideas and is still flexible enough to acknowledge that it is an evolving paradigm. From a model that was perceived as manipulative and attempting to control families it has adapted to contemporary notions characteristic of a more respectful and humble way of helping troubled families.

Practitioners are at the front line between shortcomings in social policy aspirations and the legitimate needs of families. Among a variety of methods and models of approaches and interventions modern family therapy has established itself as one of the more popular and effective tools available to practitioners. Family therapy and systems theory provide both an assessment and intervention framework for use with a range of client groups. They also offer a conceptual instrument for use outside direct contact with service users in understanding the way organisational and structural systems affect the ecology of family support practice.

This book fills a gap in the current literature available to practitioners who want to develop further knowledge and understanding of this versatile holistic approach to assessment and intervention. Family therapy is usually included in major texts as one of a range of many methods and models of practice, or it features as a subject in its own right but written for a general clinical audience. This is usually composed of psychiatrists, psychologists, nurse specialists and others embarking on advanced training to qualify as registered family therapists. Or the field is gripped by a vogue such as multi-systemic therapy. There is a need therefore for a book written by practitioners for practitioners on the subject of Family Therapy and its application to contemporary as well as future practice. This reflects the increasing popularity of the approach to family assessment and intervention, and the increased interest and development of training and accreditation in this form of psycho-social practice.

Practice application

Practitioners have traditionally expressed a keen interest in ways of working with whole families or groups in a variety of practice contexts whether in child care, child protection, mental health, community care, education, health or disability service user settings. It is widely recognised that practitioners need to develop the capacity to undertake assessments and interventions in a broad variety of settings with individuals, families, and groups. Such activity needs to be understood in the context of statutory duties, agency requirements, the needs and wishes of service users, and firmly underpinned by anti-racist and anti-discriminatory practice.

This book challenges the orthodoxy for compartmentalising practice processes that lead to narrow, resource-driven assessment procedures and eligibility criteria based on managing demand and neglecting the therapeutic dimension to practice. These managerialist processes are leading to a diminishing of the psycho-social knowledge and skill base of community family support practice. This book offers practitioners a rich source of up-to-the-minute resources to draw upon to use systems theory and the family therapy skills emanating from it to enhance a psycho-social perspective to deliver empowering, service-user focussed practice.

Recent SSI inspections and joint reviews have illustrated the need for practitioners to rediscover their core skills of assessment, so that decision-making and care-planning are based on sound analysis and understanding of the client's unique personality, history and circumstances. A systems perspective offers the most holistic tool for undertaking informed assessment work that takes into full account the wider environmental factors combined with the inter-personal relationship patterns influenc-ing family experience. Government guidance is recognising the importance of a therapeutic dimension to contemporary practice. It is beginning to be acknowledged that practitioners own therapeutic skills need to be seen as a resource to be used and offered in assessment work (DoH, 2000a).

This book will equip practitioners, students, managers and trainers with the necessary skills and understanding to harness family therapy techniques in making effective assessments, care plans, and interventions. It will enable them to explore a crucial practice resource in work with children and families and learn how the contribution of participatory practice can enrich this experience. The chapters offer theoretical and practical guidance for different interventions and approaches, and assist practitioners in considering creative ways in which these might be used in working in partnership with individuals, families, groups and the community.

Overall the book will guide practitioners through the full process from initial assessment, identification and analysis of risk, to the development, management and evaluation of intervention. It will empower practitioners to plan for non-stigmatising interventions, rooted in psycho-social principles, socially-inclusive and anti-discrim-inatory practice.

Community care reforms, childcare fiascos, and mental health panics have fuelled the drive towards a managerialist culture in practice reducing the professional autonomy of practitioners. The evidence from many practitioners is of a strong demand for the practical and theoretical resources to equip them to deal with modern family life and rediscover the value of interpersonal relationship skills. The Department of Health recently conceded that assessment processes have become de-skilling for practitioners (DoH, 2000b). This book aims to offer a knowledge and skills resources to meet that need in the context of increasing multi-disciplinary working.

Outline of the book

The book is organised for the needs of community practitioners and allied professions requiring clear, concise practice guidance in working with families or groups. Theoretical content will be kept to the minimum consistent with learning outcomes geared to competent qualifying and post-qualifying levels. Beginning with an introduction to the concept of family support and the links and connections with family therapy skills, we then examine basic theoretical foundations of the core concepts within family systems theory. The book moves through a logical progression of a description of modern methods and models, to the crucial area of socially inclusive practice. The aim is to illustrate the importance of the social context of presenting problems and the applicability of this way of working with traditionally disempowered and neglected service user groups.

Family assessment features next with contemporary guidance and support for practitioners in front line stressful situations. Ethical dilemmas in family therapy practice are discussed and analysed in order to anticipate common difficulties encountered by busy practitioners in complex situations. Family support and family group conferences are described and discussed as illustrations of realistic and achievable ways of using family therapy skills and concepts in fieldwork contexts. The final chapter examines the concept of evidence-based practice with an analysis of the effectiveness and efficiency of family therapy interventions, and the importance of evaluating practice in this therapeutic area by harnessing the capacities and strengths of families, groups – and especially taking account of the child's view of intervention.

Throughout this text readers will encounter a number of case illustrations or examples of situations involving families that we hope bring alive the subject matter. Equally we have included enough theoretical and abstract conceptual material to help you locate practical skills in authoritative evidence based knowledge. Extensive references will guide you to further reading in particular areas of interest. We aim to make this text accessible, readable and useful to a variety of practitioners seeking to help and support people with difficulties of a personal or social nature. Our definition of family embraces the widest ethnic and cultural interpretation that includes same sex partnerships, single parents, step families, kinship groups, heterosexual partnerships and marriage, extended family groupings, friendships or community living arrangements. We have deliberately used the terms therapist and practitioner interchangeably to emphasise that you do not necessarily have to embark upon family therapy training to be an effective family worker. And family therapists are not always effective family workers.

This book is our contribution to the aims for the 10th Anniversary of the International Year of the Family: 'The family constitutes the basic unit of society and therefore warrants special attention. Hence the widest possible protection and assistance should be accorded to families so that they may fully assume their responsibilities within the community, pursuant to the provisons of the Universal Declaration of Human Rights, the International Covenants on Human Rights, the Declaration on Social Progress and Development, and the Convention on the Elimination of All Forms of Discrimination against Women'.

Steven Walker
August 2004

Foreword I

This book is a welcome addition to the family therapy literature. For practitioners and other caring professionals it provides a unique overview of family therapy and its relevance to practice. For family therapists it provides an excellent exploration of the application of ideas to practice and a discussion of many of the issues and dilemmas that are raised in that process. Both authors have a strong background in both practice and research in family therapy and their experience, knowledge and skills are evident in the way in which the book explores the connections between the two.

It is evident that there are a great many overlaps and connections between family therapy values, theory and practice and the authors explore these well. For example in Chapter 1 there is a very interesting exploration of the differences and similarities between family therapy and family support.

The family is central to a great deal of government policy and caring professionals in the community are enjoined to provide support to the family in carrying out its role, and providing a strong resource for more vulnerable members. It is clear that family therapy knowledge and skills can be a significant resource in this endeavour. The authors also point out that family therapy is also concerned with the way in which environmental and other contextual factors can influence the capacity of families to function well and to make necessary changes. Along with all practitioners family therapists are interested in social justice as well as social care.

Over the past forty years there have been major developments in the fields of family support and family therapy. One criticism of family support is that under the mantle of a huge and impossible task it has become more management focussed and has lost some of the therapeutic richness that existed previously. Indeed there was a period in the eighties and nineties when social work for example was being pulled out of NHS settings to meet the heavy child protection demand in the community. It was at this point that some practitioners managed to negotiate employment by the health service and those trained in family therapy became family therapists. In many instances they found that their job was not much different although they had changed employer and profession! I make this point only to emphasise the close and complex relationship that exists. If we map theoretical and value developments in both fields there are many similarities. For example the interest in post-modernism, in collaborative practice, in user involvement and social justice issues. Anti-discriminatory practice and an awareness of the rich variety of family forms that exist in society are shared by both. They also both address issues of power prejudice and discrimination which impact on all our lives. Another shared area of interest is in the need to develop an evidence base for practice. This is an area where there could be more sharing of ideas and resources.

The authors also explore some of the differences and more problematic aspects of the relationship. These include misperceptions on both sides and this exploration creates a very useful frame for the content of the book. However family therapy has a specific focus on how people change or get stuck in their journey through life and one of the values of systems and narrative theories is that they provide frameworks for changing behaviour, beliefs and relationships in a way that helps families to move forward in a more positive way for their members. Because the theory can be applied to all levels of context it is easy to include professional and community and wider systems in the whole picture surrounding a named client.

There are many strengths to this book and these will become evident to the reader. However I think that it is useful to highlight a few aspects of the book that particularly impressed me. I really liked the way in which the authors managed to provide a broad overview of theoretical and practice developments over time in a very clear way. Throughout the book they keep the discussion entirely relevant to professional practice and there is a continuous referencing to family support and family therapy. This is aided by a wealth of useful case illustrations and there are full and useful guides to further reading.

The chapter on socially inclusive practice and social policy will be useful for all mental health and social service practitioners. There is a very useful and well developed chapter on attachment theory which will certainly be of great interest to family therapists as well as practitioners. The application of systems ideas to assessment is well developed in the area of children and families and the authors focus specifically on the McMaster model of assessing family functioning. This has a great deal to offer and again will also be of interest and use to family therapists, especially those in training. As one would expect from a book of this calibre there is a strong section on the ethics of working with families and a final section addresses the issues, dilemmas and possibilities of evaluating effectiveness.

Congratulations to Steven Walker and Jane Akister in producing such a well researched and academically sound book which is great to read and continually links theory to practice. This will certainly make a significant contribution to the training literature for all practitioners and family therapists and also help more experienced practitioners to develop their practice. In the Association for Family Therapy we have the major aim of working to improve the therapeutic services to families and include members who are trained as family therapists but also those who have an interest and commitment to work with families in any capacity.

Judith Lask Chair of Association for Family Therapy
March 2004

Foreword 2

About fifteen years ago I attended a workshop given by one of the major figures in the development of family therapy, Lynn Hoffman. During her presentation she made a point that some of the most interesting developments in the utilisation of family therapy ideas were being developed in Britain. In particular, she made a distinction between being a family therapist, and using family therapy ideas in the primary context in which one worked. Amongst the contexts she talked about was social work and other caring professions. One of her central points was that, while we may train people to be specialists in family therapy, family therapy would be of little use if its ideas were not part of a much wider vision. Salvador Minuchin, another of the major figures in the development of family therapy also made a similar point at a conference a couple of years ago in Melbourne, Australia.

It was the application of family therapy ideas across professions such as social work, while not subverting those professions, that so impressed people such as Lynn Hoffman. Indeed, in the mid 1990s The Association of Family Therapy changed its name to The Association for Family Therapy and Systemic Practice in the UK. This was, in part, in recognition of the fact that many caring professionals such as practitioners were, increasingly, using family therapy ideas in their work without wanting to see themselves as family therapists. The Association for Family Therapy thus recognised that the emphasis for some professionals was more on systemic thinking and practice rather than family therapy and that the Association needed to be more inclusive of those professionals. This book then, is a timely and interesting contribution to this development of inclusiveness.

In a very clear outline of their rationale for the writing of the book, the authors, Jane Akister and Steven Walker make a very important point. They say that the book 'challenges the orthodoxy for compartmentalising practice processes that lead to narrow, resource-driven assessment procedures and eligibility criteria based on managing demand and **neglecting the therapeutic dimension to practice**' (my emphasis) (introduction). They rightly, I think, believe that there has been a 'diminishing of the psycho-social knowledge and skill base of professional practice.' (ibid).

Family support had, for many years, a reputation for skills based therapeutic work. This, however, was never enough and marginalised wider discourses around social inequality. In seeking to redress this neglect the therapeutic dimension to practice itself became marginalised. Therapeutic work, more and more, moved into the domain of specialists and generic work suffered in terms of its ownership of a therapeutic dimension to practice.

One of the strengths of this book is that it seeks to bring together issues of social inequality and the therapeutic dimension rather than see them as somehow mutually exclusive – a both/and rather than an either/or position. They do this by outlining how family therapy developments have, in the last 15 years, paid much more attention to issues of gender, race, culture, ethnicity, inclusiveness, collaborative approaches and evidence based practice and how therapeutic skills have developed to include these issues in face to face practice.

It seems to me, also, that through re-highlighting the need for more attention to be made to therapeutic skills in practice with children and families, the authors are making an important point in this book about the ownership of expertise. Perhaps more specifically, they advocate the reclaiming of some of the skills that have perhaps become marginalised in the caring professions. This book will be a helpful guide for those who want to think more about how to use systems ideas in their practice.

Dr Barry Mason Director The Institute of Family Therapy, London

About the Authors

Steven Walker completed his Masters degree in social work at the London School of Economics then worked in voluntary and statutory contexts in inner London and Essex for 15 years. He practised in generic and specialist settings specialising in child protection and child and adolescent mental health. In 1992 he qualified as a family psychotherapist after training at the Tavistock Institute and the Institute of Family Therapy.

Jane Akister completed her Masters degree at Oxford University then trained in family therapy and practised in psychiatric social work in Newcastle and Manchester. She worked for 8 years at the MRC unit on the integration and development of behaviour at Cambridge University. Her current research interests are in child protection and parenting.

Acknowledgements

Staff at the Tavistock Institute and the Institute of Family Therapy have been influential in developing our practice in family therapy.

We would like to thank particularly Barry Mason, Jane Dutton, Annie Turner, Hugh Jenkins, David Campbell, Judith Lask, Robin Skynner, Myrna Gower, Charlotte Burck, Stephen Frosh, Damian McCann, Pete Short, and Andy Treacher.

Many thanks to Nate Epstein, Duane Bishop, Gabor Keitner and Ian Goodyer for their help and support over many years. Any omissions are not a reflection of the importance of any individuals' part in our development or as the source of inspiration for some of the book's contents, but rather the limits of space and memory.

Clients, colleagues and the many students at Anglia Polytechnic University have provided us with an enormous resource from which to draw in constructing this book and ensuring its relevance to contemporary practice. We thank them especially. All case illustrations have been anonymised and details changed to protect confidentiality.

Our own families past and present, are of course probably the foundational influence in our interest and thinking on family life and in how to help when difficulties are experienced. They are our living testimony to the rich variety of positive and negative experiences within which we have grown physically and emotionally, and where we have learned the value of kinship relationships that can offer a secure, supportive, unconditional attachment from which to manage life's challenges. To them this book is dedicated with our love.

CHAPTER I

Family Support and Family Therapy

Introduction

Working with families has always been a core task of practitioners and other professionals whether in community care, child care, or mental health services. The family is the forum for many of the psycho-social dramas that unfold in the everyday working lives of practitioners in statutory, voluntary or independent contexts. It is little wonder therefore that staff demand the knowledge and skills to assess and intervene competently in this human arena in order to maximise the help and support to service users, carers, children and parents. Many practitioners have undertaken foundation, intermediate or advanced training in **family therapy** as a means of equipping themselves to face the increasingly complex and demanding nature of modern practice.

Many practitioners undertake different post-qualifying training in a variety of ways as part of Continuous Professional Development. This may involve specific child protection training or group work skills or specific therapeutic techniques such as **cognitive behavioural** or **solution-focussed therapy**. Whether the training is called family therapy or something else they are both in some way or another going to support families with problems. The old joke about which came first, the chicken or the egg, can be applied to **family therapy** and **family support** as a way of addressing an important issue about the relationship between different ways of helping families.

Addressing the question offers an opportunity to consider the differences and the similarities between family support and family therapy. In so doing it can help demystify and illuminate the most appropriate resources required by practitioners, and explore ways in which practitioners tasked with a range of service users can practice in thoughtful, rigorous and sensitive ways. While few practitioners are employed as family therapists a great many in family support roles will be using similar techniques and strategies consistent with the systems theory that underpins family therapy practice. Practitioners in a variety of contexts will characterise their work according to a range of criteria drawing on theoretical resources that serve to justify certain activities.

Family support can be perceived as an overall aspiration within which particular models and techniques of practice are employed. These models and methods can be rooted in behavioural, psycho-dynamic or task centred theories and focus on individuals, couples or the whole family. Family therapists using systems theory might also characterise their work in terms of a range of methods including for example, structural, psycho-analytic, systemic, cognitive-behavioural, and solution-focussed or constructionist. Equally, the focus can be on the individual, couple or whole family. Figure 1.1 illustrates the overlap and interconnectedness between the methods employed, models of practice and the focus of intervention.

Within each overall mode of working there are a wide variety of techniques and approaches. So when terms such as family support and family therapy are used in multi-disciplinary professional

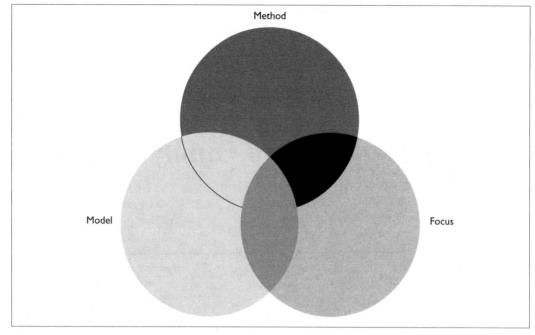

Figure 1.1: The overlap of methods employed, models of practice and the focus of intervention

contexts such as inter-agency meetings or case conferences it would not be surprising if participants made a number of different assumptions about what was actually being proposed or had already been tried in practice. Without clarification about what these terms mean the potential for confusion is high as well as the possibility that families receive mixed messages and conflicting advice.

Both terms use the word **family** and that can, in itself, be misleading, if there are a number of assumptions about what a family is. Traditional definitions were very narrow and reflected an era when a heterosexual couple married, had children, and lived under the same roof. Nowadays this nuclear family stereotype is surprisingly resilient despite evidence of the diversity of different forms of family life. This popular conception of how the family is constituted is more a reflection of how some traditionalists believe sexual, emotional and parental relationships *ought* to be structured (Muncie and Sapsford, 1997).

In contemporary multi-cultural society with a rich tapestry of ethnic diversity combined with rapid sociological transformations there are a wide and complex variety of 'families' such as extended, kin group, and lone parent. These can be further distinguished by parental partnerships which may or may not be same sex couples, cohabiting, adoptive, fostering, separated, divorced, remarried, or step-parents. Stretching the definition of family further can include the important role that peers, friends and local community figures perform in shaping and influencing family patterns of behaviour. We can therefore see that apparently simple words such as **family** and **support** or **therapy** are complex concepts bearing closer examination.

This is important in the context of finding ways of working that are relevant and acceptable to service users. Family support has had, for example, to adapt its historical focus on the traditional nuclear family model, whereas the more recent practice of family therapy has had to consider the effectiveness of culturally-competent methods of working with different family forms, rather than trying to defend its focus on systems rather than individuals. Indeed there is a creative body of literature developing that illustrates how family therapy concepts can be adapted for work with individuals or couples. For example family therapy skills are being adapted for individual work with children (Wilson, 1999).

Some literature identifies the use to which family therapy ideas have been put, but the influences are described in a **linear**, rather than **circular** direction (Treacher and Carpenter, 1984; Kelsall and McCullough, 1988; Manor, 1991). Family therapists usually eschew the notion of linearity. On the other hand studies of the effectiveness of family support use systemic concepts such as circularity very similar to the most orthodox family therapist (Gardner, 1998; Hellinckx et al., 1997; Pinkerton et al., 2000). Family support therefore may have something to offer family therapy and vice versa.

In a similar way to the silent discourse between feminism and family therapy that was eventually heard, there seems to be a contemporary lack of dialogue between those practising family therapy and those engaged in family support. Family support tends to be marginalised as an activity without a clear definition, whereas family therapy has spawned specialist journals and requires advanced clinical qualifications for specific occupational roles. Feminist family therapists began to realise that family therapy was failing to engage with feminist ideas of women's unequal position in the family structure. Practice seemed to be based on a denial of the unequal power relationships underpinning family dynamics and was therefore not truly systemic (Hare-Mustin, 1978; Goldner, 1985; Walker, 2003a).

Any discussion of the family nowadays which omits the dimension of gender power would be considered inadequate, especially in the context of child and family work where practitioners need to fully understand how masculine power is used in overt and covert ways to control, dominate and abuse partners and children. As public and professional debate constantly agonises over the emotional health of families and how to improve it, family therapy and family support are expanding their reach in the arena of family welfare policy and practice (Gorrell Barnes, 1998; Statham, 2000). Both aspire to improving practice and engaging in evidence-based evaluation. Both are sometimes perceived as descriptions of therapeutic practice and service delivery format.

Yet there is an absence of open discussion between the two interventions and an unspoken assumption that family support is for the working class practised by unqualified or low-paid generic staff, while family therapy is for the middle classes and practised by highly paid post-qualified specialists. By opening up the dialogue between them, it may be possible for practitioners to engage in a mutual learning process to benefit one another, as well as individual and family clients or service users.

The question of status

Family support appears to have been ascribed a low priority on the statutory health and social care agenda in the United Kingdom. This is evidenced by several things including increased pressure to improve child protection investigations, retrenchment in statutory preventive services, and the encouragement of charitable and non-governmental family support services (DoH, 1999). Meanwhile family therapy enjoys a privileged position within the regulatory United Kingdom Council for Psychotherapy and is developing a professional status distinct from its practitioner roots in social work, psychology or nursing. Therefore the status and perception of both family therapy and family support are important issues to consider.

Fiscal and structural changes in the funding and organisation of social and health care are forcing choices about where to target finite resources to help families in need. Statutory workers bemoan the lack of time to practice preventively and at the same time are unable to employ therapeutic methods once problems arise because of the crisis-driven nature of cases which militate against establishing a safe, containing therapeutic relationship. Thresholds for eligibility criteria to services are so restricted that only the most worrying cases with high levels of risk tend to be accepted into statutory services.

Recently renewed interest in early intervention and preventive practice in the context of reliable evidence has enabled close examination of the challenges in assessing needs and demand against resource constraints (Tunstill, 1996; Thoburn et al., 1998). Within government policy changes there is a possible ambivalence about the status and priority of family support work in the

United Kingdom, and noted elsewhere (Hell-inckx et al., 1997). Family support can be perceived as something any well-meaning person can provide while family therapy is elevated to the rarefied status of advanced professionalism. Yet they are both operating in very similar domains and can use similar therapeutic concepts with parallel processes and outcomes.

There has been growing professional and public concern in recent years about the rising trends in children's emotional and behavioural problems. This has prompted health and social policy responses to the growing demand for child and adolescent mental health services in the United Kingdom and elsewhere (Rutter and Smith, 1995; Audit Commission, 1998; Mental Health Foundation, 1999; Micklewright and Stewart, 2000; Singh et al., 2000; Walker, 2001a). One of the issues raised is where and how to focus limited staffing and therapeutic resources to help families in trouble (DoH, 1997c, 1998b). A wider issue concerns the purpose of intervention in families – whether it is family support or family therapy.

Both could be held to be trying to endorse and shore up an anachronistic social organisation if their stated aim is to maintain family functioning and prevent family disintegration. On the other hand, a more neutral stance would aim to provide families with a helping context and empowering resources. With these the family is able to embark on a transformational experience that could include separation or continuation, with interventions that are deliberately not privileging one form of living arrangement over any other. Practitioners will be familiar with the dilemma of trying to maintain a current family organisation while balancing the short and long term risks of removing children, or seeking an injunction against an abusive father.

The upward trend in child and adolescent mental health problems and specific increases in young male suicides, school behavioural problems, and female eating disorders provide examples of situations where issues about the focus of intervention and the form of intervention require serious attention. Are these manifestations of something inherently wrong with the modern family or are they the social consequences of the impact of free market economic expansion? In

other words should practitioners be trying to help parents cope better with the emotional and behavioural needs of a new generation of children and young people, or help families challenge the prevailing socio-economic structures that produce such negative effects?

It is argued that market discipline and regimes have had a significant impact on welfare provisions in the industrialised world and have contributed substantially to redrawing the role of the state, particularly with regards to the provision of welfare resources. As the limitations of capitalist *laissez faire* economics are revealed by unemployment and massive differences in wealth between countries, so global opposition to the social and psychological consequences increases. Practitioners can assist in mobilising people who seek to liberate and empower themselves and orient their activities in providing assistance for one another and meeting their collective welfare needs (Dominelli, 2002).

The social policy context

Family support was part of the early intervention of charity organisations and hospital almoners who were the forerunners of modern practitioners. Until the early part of the twentieth century when psychoanalytic ideas and the therapeutic movement began to influence the emerging profession of social work, family support *was* social work. The family has always been an important locus of intervention but this systemic focus was eclipsed by psycho-dynamic casework oriented towards the individual. This occurred at the same time as psychiatry began to develop as a profession with interest in the effectiveness of psycho-therapeutic, as opposed to pharmacological interventions. Practitioners employed in secondary mental health settings were especially influenced by these developments.

In the 1950s family therapy ideas began to permeate professional practice and started to occupy the space left by social work (Wood, 1980). A long history of interest and concern by welfare policy makers influenced by studies of family life can be traced to contemporary evidence providing a developing picture of changing family characteristics which have accelerated over the past thirty years (Kay-Shuttleworth, 1832; Leslie and Morton, 2001; NCH Action for Children, 2000; DoH, 1997; Utting, 1995).

The consequent increased volume, complexity, and severity of child and adolescent mental health problems has attracted much more recent concern (Webster-Stratton, 1997; Gordon and Grant, 1997; Walker, 1999; Carr, 2000). The rising trend in divorce, increase in single parent households, stepfamilies, and increased cohabitation, have contributed to a sense of structural change in the pattern of contemporary family relationships. These trends have placed families, and the need to find the most effective ways of helping them, at the centre of an important debate.

The widening gap between rich and poor highlights the needs of those families who are socially excluded, marginalised and disempowered. Increased numbers of mothers in work, the ageing of the population, the rise in youth homelessness, increased reporting of domestic violence, child abuse, and the prevalence of substance misuse, are all cited as evidence of the pressures and strains put on modern family life. The political debate divides between those who blame lax child-rearing practices and the permissive 1960s, and those who blame the growth of individualism and the failures of capitalist economics to fulfil society's welfare needs.

Racism and xenophobia have increased as European Union enlargement has accelerated migration, armed conflict has precipitated increased numbers of asylum seekers, and economic and social dislocation has prompted more refugee applications to wealthier countries (Walker, 2002). Communities which are already impoverished have been incited to regard families fleeing persecution, ethnic cleansing and political oppression as an unwelcome burden and part of the problem. These changes in the socio-geographic texture of Europe are mirrored in other countries producing similar moral panics and hasty policy changes to tackle the consequences.

Issues of citizenship and nationality, race and immigration provide the overarching context within legislation and public policy which sets the scene for racist and oppressive practice to go unchecked. The British Nationality Act (HMSO, 1948) provided legal rights to immigration which

have served as a focal point for a continuing racialised debate about the numbers of black immigrants and refugees or asylum seekers and the perceived social problems subsequently caused. The Race Relations (Amendment) Act (HMSO, 2000) came into force in 2001 extending the scope of the Race Relations Act (HMSO, 1976). The new Act strengthens the law in two ways that are significant to practice:

- It extends protection against racial discrimination by public authorities.
- It places a new, enforceable positive duty on public authorities.

Like the Human Rights Act (UN, 1998) the new Act defines a *public authority* very widely. Anyone whose work involves functions of a public nature must not discriminate on racial grounds while carrying out those functions. The most important aspect of the new Act in the long term will be the new positive duty on local authorities because it gives statutory force to the imperative of tackling institutional racism. The new general duty replaces section 71 of the Race Relations Act 1976 with a tougher requirement on public authorities to eliminate unlawful discrimination and promote equality of opportunity and good race relations in carrying out their functions. Thus family support and family therapy intervention must reflect anti-racist and anti-oppressive values.

At the 1991 census just over 3 million (5.5 per cent) of the 55 million people in Britain did not classify themselves as white. Half are South Asian (that is, of Indian, Pakistani, and Bangladeshi descent) and 30 per cent are black. The rich diversity of Britain's minority populations reveals that nearly half of Britain's non-white population had been born in Britain, with three-quarters of these registered British citizens. The overwhelming majority of non-white children under 16 were therefore born in Britain.

The Nationality, Immigration and Asylum Bill (HMSO, 2002) is the fourth piece of primary legislation attempting to reform the asylum system in 10 years. Previous measures related to dispersal and support measures and were widely regarded as harmful to family and children's health because they resulted in sub-standard accommodation, isolation, discrimination and poverty (Dennis and Smith, 2002; JCWI, 2002). The new law proposes the establishment of accommodation centres housing about 3,000 people in rural areas. Protection of children in such places will be difficult due to the high turnover of residents, while these children will be deprived of opportunities to integrate and feel part of society.

In addition, the new law proposes denying asylum-seeking children the right to be educated in mainstream local schools. Such segregation could contravene the Human Rights Act 1998 and the UN Convention on the Rights of the Child (UN, 1989) because this is not in the best interests of the child and will very likely harm their development and mental health. Children who have suffered extreme trauma, anxiety and hardship, need to feel safe, included and part of their new community with their peers in order to begin to thrive and rebuild their fragile mental health. There are serious doubts that the quality of education offered in accommodation centres would properly meet even basic standards of pedagogic practice (Walker, 2003).

The proposals in the law on marriage and family visits are another potential source of anxiety and psychological harm to children and young people. The subject of arranged marriage combines further attempts to restrict entry from abroad with a barely disguised racist attack on cultural practices in some black communities. A two-year probationary period for marriages is proposed in order to test the integrity of individuals who enter into marriages abroad with non-British citizens. The effect will be to increase the number of children confronting the prospect of separation from one parent because of doubts raised about whether their parents' marriage will subsist indefinitely. Culturally competent practice is required from practitioners engaged in family support work or practising family therapy.

Recent research on child poverty ranked Britain bottom in a comparison of the current fifteen European Union countries with 32 per cent of children living in poor households (Micklewright and Stewart, 2000). This is an important part of the equation of demand, needs, and resources when evaluating provision. It has

long been argued that early intervention is the key to effectiveness because it stops problems getting worse when they become harder to tackle. It is less costly in terms of damage to children's development, family relationships, use of scarce resources, and prevention of anti-social consequences in the long-term (Bayley, 1999). However, Eayrs and Jones (1992) have pointed out that the accumulated evidence for the effectiveness of early intervention programmes is not as optimistic as was once hoped. On occasion there is the possibility that such programmes can be damaging, de-skilling, and undermining of parents confidence.

On the other hand a meta-analysis of early education interventions demonstrated that children from disadvantaged backgrounds were less at risk from developing maladjustment, school failure and delinquency after participating in these programmes which were delivered in an educational context (Sylva, 1994). Though yet to be researched fully, premarital counselling is a preventive focus which offers the chance for couples to enhance problem-solving and decision-making skills (Stahmann, 2000). Some outcome research on primary prevention mental health programmes focussed on school-based activities and concluded that positive changes were reported in social adjustment, academic performance, and cognitive skills leading to a reduction in mental health problems (Durlak, 1998). The location of family support is clearly critical in engaging parents and children. Schools are emerging as an acceptable and accessible non-stigmatising venue for individual or group-based activity where attached practitioners using systems concepts can engage in inter-professional work.

Definitions and distinctions

Family support can be defined as self-help or volunteer help with little statutory involvement, or it can mean a continuum of advice, support, and specialist help geared to provide early preventive intervention. The intervention can be directed at individual parents, couples, the child, the whole family, or in groups. It can consist of individual counselling, psychotherapy, group work, advice and information, or the provision of practical help. Within the mix of interventions are the hallmarks of the family therapy paradigm that assumes problems are manifested within interpersonal relationships that are themselves part of a wider social context.

The status and perception of preventive family support work can be usefully conceptualised using a three-stage model identifying different levels of intervention (Hardiker, 1995). The **primary level** offers universally available services that can strengthen family functioning and is provided by a mix of state welfare providers and parent education services often organised by voluntary organisations. The **secondary level** provides services targeted on families in early difficulties such as relationship counselling for couples, informal family centres, and home visiting schemes by voluntary agencies to help families with young children.

At the **third or tertiary level**, work with families can include those who are suffering severe difficulties and on the threshold of care proceedings characterised by intensive work either by the statutory or voluntary sector to prevent family breakdown. Services geared towards the needs of specific age groups of children or young people, or adults can determine the type of help offered and whether it is perceived as family or individual support (Walker, 2001b). At each level family therapists and family support workers can become involved with the same families.

Family therapy has evolved into something which bears many definitions, ranging from simple ones which offer a view of problems as inter-personal rather than individual (Dallos and Draper, 2000) to comprehensive ones like Gorell-Barnes (1998) who describes the activities as:

- Encompassing a philosophy of relational events.
- Methods of description between people and their social context.
- A relational approach to work with families.
- A variety of therapeutic methods.

Some of the literature on family support describes ways of helping families (Sutton, 1999; Hill, 1999; Pinkerton et al., 2000). They provide the following common characteristics:

- Using listening skills.
- Getting alongside families.
- Emphasising collaboration.
- Developing cultural awareness.
- Gathering information.
- Recognising positives in the situation.

An examination of these terms quickly shows similarities with skills considered important for family therapy training and accreditation, and will be familiar to those undertaking foundation level training in family support even though different vocabulary is employed. How far support or therapy directly address the social context, or succeed in doing so is a moot point. The debate about the fit between family therapy practice and its application in social policy contexts has generated thoughtful contributions (Berger and Jurkovic, 1984; Campbell and Draper, 1985; Reimers and Treacher, 1995; Sveaass and Reichelt, 2001; Papadopoulos, 2001). The most recent contributions focus on the socio-political discourse generated around refugees and asylum seekers, and how these meta-contexts invariably intrude on the therapeutic encounter.

Families from areas of conflict will encounter family therapy or family support services, particularly when the effects of trauma manifest in mental health problems. Without an active engagement with the social policy context that portrays these families as objects of pity or welfare scroungers, therapists and support staff can limit their helping potential. It could be argued that family support services by their very nature, would be oriented more towards this social policy context, and are created to specifically address issues raised within it.

But they may be missing important 'therapeutic' opportunities that are masked by too narrow a focus on human rights, legal, or welfare benefit tasks. On the other hand, family therapists employing an inflexible therapeutic model, and concentrating on the intra-familial beliefs, behaviour and patterns of communication, might be missing an important 'social' dimension to the family's experience and neglecting to find culturally competent ways of engaging them. The use of interpreters adds yet another complication where communication becomes more and more difficult as each person in the process seeks to interpret others beliefs whilst not necessarily making their own explicit.

Families and practitioners

Early research on practitioners using family therapy ideas in their work with families showed the following reasons for valuing such an approach (Gorell-Barnes, 1984):

- The method offered an open model of communication and sharing which was enjoyed by the family.
- The method was enjoyed by the practitioner.
- It moved the focus of concern from the individual to the family with positive results.
- It offered a realistic way of working.
- It was effective in problem solving compared to other methods.
- It improved the quality of family life in addition to problem solving.

One of the problems practitioners encounter in engaging with families in a statutory context and trying to employ family therapy methods is the threat they pose to families where the prospect of relationship changes is more overwhelming than the removal and institutionalisation of one of its members. The pattern of contact with social services may have been one of child protection or child care activity requiring the use of statutory powers to intervene. This 'resistance' to change is at the heart of all therapeutic paradigms as well as family support services. Unfortunately this can also confirm a partial systems view that an individual needs to be sacrificed or scapegoated by a dysfunctional family, rather than everyone concerned engaging in familial change.

However, family therapists can use the concept of reframing the behaviour and the beliefs, informing it as a means of illustrating the powerful protective forces at work inside families. In other words the acceptance by some individuals to being labelled as 'the problem' can be perceived as a means of protecting the family status quo. Suggesting to a family that the problem behaviour is serving a protective or loving function on behalf of other members, is a strong message. This also testifies to the intrinsic strengths in a family who have developed such loyalty in one of their members, strengths which may have been temporarily lost sight of during the crisis (Gorell-Barnes, 1984).

Practitioners using this notion outside a formal clinical or therapeutic work setting will find it challenging in busy children-and-families teams where despite government policy directives to the contrary, because the climate is one of time constraints and resource shortages, investigation and assessment are the priority. This creates in the worker a reduction in expectations and a feeling of impotence and disempowerment that is invariably transmitted to clients. The family then have to acquire the variety of labels that trigger intervention such as 'in need' or 'dysfunctional' where the opportunities for building on their strengths and resourcefulness are blighted. Both practitioner and service user are thus restricted within circumscribed roles that militate against a positive partnership engaged in problem-solving activity.

Some family centres come closer to achieving the goal of offering a resource with a range of user-focussed services such as advocacy, group work, support groups, individual counselling, and couples and family therapy. Such centres it is argued are better equipped to provide a more comprehensive service to disadvantaged users than for example, child and family consultation services staffed by professionals who have a narrower range of predominantly clinical skills (Reimers and Treacher, 1995). Family centres are less stigmatising, they tend to have active representation from service users in the way they are run, and with clients who are motivated to attend, they ironically create the ideal conditions for effective therapeutic outcomes.

Case illustration

The M family were referred to the child care team following a period of increasing concern about the parents' capacity to cope with multiple problems including: unemployment, financial shortages, overcrowding, husband's violent temper, female teenager depressed and refusing school, and two children under five demonstrating attachment difficulties. The case was allocated to a practitioner who made an initial assessment and then combined this with the extensive history from the case record to produce an action plan. The evidence suggested that the family had never received consistent or coherent support, but reactive service based on superficial negative risk assessments and anxieties generated by health and school staff.

Commentary

In order to make a difference and respond in another way rather than that anticipated by other people including the family themselves, the practitioner using a systems approach could begin by discussing options with all the family members present. This in itself would be unique because previously, for various reasons, the social work staff had only met with Mrs M. Taking the trouble to arrange a whole family meeting immediately changes the context for the practitioner's visit. This permits each person to voice (or draw in the case of the under-5s) their perception of the family situation. This sets the scene for the work to follow and ensures that everyone has a stake in the process.

There are a number of options once agreement has been reached about the practical ways of addressing the problems as defined by the family. Individual contact may need to be included especially if there are concerns about abuse or domestic violence. Another worker can help in this respect with the double advantage of providing the caseworker with additional support and another resource for certain members of the family – e.g. a male practitioner to meet with Mr M or a health visitor to do some parent modelling with Mrs M. A family centre could be contracted to do a number of sessions with various combinations of the family system, including extended family or friends.

A time-limited period of contact with a verbal or written agreement with a proper assessment and report at the end composed in partnership with the whole family, demonstrates a different type of engagement with the M family. Using systems theory and family therapy techniques will help the allocated worker maintain a broad perspective of the family as an interactive system, rather than focussing narrowly on individual problems. Blame and scapegoating are avoided and the opportunities for change are maximised. Nevertheless, a professional practitioner will need to anticipate a potential failure in this strategy and prepare for matters to worsen that require a more statutory or directive approach if risks increase and care diminishes.

The needs of families

There has always been an interest among health and social care professionals, and voluntary agency staff, in providing earlier and more appropriate support to families where help with children is needed. This can assist in preventing more serious problems, or to deflect the need for statutory intervention (Baradon et al., 1999; Gardner, 1998; Gibbons and Wilding, 1995; Iwaniec, 1995).

Together with rapid sociological change affecting the ability of parents to cope without traditional kinship support, the issue of family support continues to be highlighted, but at the same time surrounded by different definitions and strategies. An examination of the characteristics of models of assessment, analysis of methods of support, and evaluation of measures of effectiveness, permits some comparisons to be drawn between family therapy and family support and how they best meet the needs of families.

The family therapy literature is limited on the subject of pro-active community involvement and a social dimension to practice, beyond rhetorical injunctions to address oppressive and discriminatory contexts of lived experience in codes of conduct and ethical guidance. Family therapists have largely failed to integrate a thorough social policy perspective with their theoretical paradigms by remaining disconnected from the communities they aspire to help (Doherty and Beaton, 2000).

These criticisms rely on a rather narrow and impatiently explicit concept of social action. It may be that the subtle and more implicit benefits of family therapy practice are not visible to conventional research methodologies. The concept of more collaborative, client-centred, community-oriented practice in family therapy is echoed in some contemporary writings (Reimers and Treacher, 1995; Anderson, 1997; Anderson, 2001). They also actually have a robust historical pedigree with evidence that the pioneering family therapists were more focussed on the needs of impoverished communities and employing strategies to explicitly address the social context of family problems (Bell, 1961; Minuchin, 1974).

Feminist family therapists have contributed valued thinking regarding one of the most important social contexts of family therapy practice – that of gender, which is not inconsistent with the aims of staff working in family support where they are generally helping women (Perelberg and Miller, 1990). Relatively new literature is responding to earlier criticisms about family therapy's notorious resistance to tackle issues of culture, race, and sexuality (Long, 1996; Lau, 1988; McGoldrick et al., 1982; Hardy and Laszloffy, 1994). It is as if family therapists are less defensive about their theoretical and philosophical beliefs and practices, and having recently established a presence within the therapeutic community, are now able to let go of ideological purity and engage with the messiness of contemporary families lived experiences.

Studies into the effectiveness of family support or family therapy evidence impact at the micro and macro level of intervention context and the subtle interaction between both levels (Estrada and Pinsof, 1995; Hill, 1999). Apart from registering success with the external parent-child relationship, findings suggest impact at the internal intra-psychic relationships. Thus the parent's internal representation of their child is changed and the child's internal representation of its' mother can be changed. In other words, practitioners operating in either mode are finding additional benefits to the intended outcomes of intervention. Therapists are helping families in the wider context while support staff are witnessing subtle changes in the quality of relationships.

The concept of the shaman illustrates this when describing the therapist as a figure who intervenes at the junction between different orders of reality – the physiological, psychological, and social (Wiseman, 1999). The blurring of these distinctions and the interactive nature of their process requires a creative synthesising of skills, theory,

and applied knowledge. A broad repertoire of therapeutic modalities including cognitive, behavioural, systemic, psycho-dynamic, solution-focussed approaches have demonstrated positive outcome in a range of presenting problems in a variety of specialist, statutory, or voluntary, community settings (Fuchs, 1995; Carr, 2000).

A review of the literature on empirical evaluations of family support services yielded mixed results, and conceded that the disparate number of variables affecting outcome makes it difficult to isolate the particular impact of such an intervention (Rossi, 1992). Other research notes that family support programmes tend to focus on single outcome measures related to a child's behaviour, rather than taking into account other dimensions such as parent/child interaction or use of community resources (Gardner, 1998).

A review of consumer studies of family therapy concluded that the importance of the relationship aspects of therapy were crucial as far as service users were concerned (Reimers and Treacher, 1995). Active elements such as advice-giving need to be combined with reflective and supportive elements as is the case in family support work. The concepts, practices and outcomes of family therapy and family support are therefore not as incompatible as might at first appear.

Family support provides individual, parent, couple, and groupwork interventions to referred children and families because of concerns about the emotional and behavioural development of children. Evidence from similar initiatives suggests that Family Support could provide valuable support to socially excluded children and families (Davis et al., 1997; Arcelus et al., 1999).

The multi-faceted approach to assessment common to both family therapy and family support interventions is consistent with the recently introduced *Framework for the Assessment of Children in Need* which requires professionals working with children to expand the focus of their assessments in order to improve decision-making (DoH, 2000). This framework also explicitly acknowledges environmental factors and the wider social context in the analysis of children and family difficulties.

The aim of this government policy guidance is to try to move away from the much-criticised intrusive and inspectorial style of assessment of families where there were concerns about the welfare of children. Social work practitioners are required to make comprehensive assessments of all the variables affecting the functioning of the family not relying on a narrow focus on any one of the three key assessment areas: parenting, environment, or child development.

The model of assessment has all the characteristics of a psycho-social, holistic, and participative, approach, maintaining the focus towards intervention that is appropriate, accessible, and acceptable to children and parents. Again, the similarities with a family therapy service are close. One of the key characteristics of family support services is the partnership approach to work with service users. This is often enshrined in a process of negotiation with families about the venue for work, and the choice of practice methods, during the assessment process. This echoes some of the social constructionist ideas in family therapy discourse (White and Epston, 1990; Hoffman, 1993; White, 1995).

Family support skills ranged from cognitive-behavioural, brief therapy, counselling, narrative, and systemic approaches, through to groupwork, task-centred work, or advice and information giving. These methods and models are echoed throughout the Family Therapy theoretical and practice literature (Bentovim et al., 1982; Gurman and Kniskern, 1991; Dallos and Draper, 2000).

An important similarity between family therapy and family support is the way they inadvertently replicate another social structure which obscures the rights of children, especially in the area of child and adolescent mental health (Walker, 2001b). Children's perspectives have rarely been explored in relation to the help they receive towards their emotional and mental well-being (Hill et al., 1995; Gordon and Grant, 1997). Few studies have been undertaken with regard to therapeutic interventions with children and young people experiencing emotional and behavioural difficulties and whether they found the therapy helpful. This is a serious omission in the evidence base for practice improvement, and at variance with the contemporary interest on children's rights as service users.

Those that have been undertaken have found that generally children speak less than parents when interviewed together, while adolescents express themselves in limited ways tending to agree or disagree. Therapists spoke more often to parents than to children when attempting to evaluate the help and support offered (Marshal et al., 1989; Friedlander et al., 1985; Cederborg, 1997). Evidence of children's desire to be part of therapy suggests that children's reactions to therapy are influenced by their attachment style (Smith et al., 1996; Strickland-Clark et al., 2000). In families where there are insecure attachments for example, children can feel constrained to speak more freely because of fears of what the consequences might be and the discomfort in exposing painful or difficult feelings. There is no reason to suppose the same dynamics do not operate in family support work, where children's perspectives may also be neglected.

Family therapy or family support?

Does it matter what the work is called if all the stakeholders are satisfied? Wide status and pay differentials between qualified family therapists working in mental health services and family support workers employed by voluntary agencies do matter to staff. They often work with the same families and these differentials can cause envy, which will impact on relationships between staff in different positions. This must therefore impact on the work with clients or service users.

Equally, some families are intimidated by the concept of therapy, combined with the mental illness connotations and the stigma of child and adolescent mental health services, which can be strongly influenced by a medical, rather than social model of psychiatry. Other families are flattered by the opportunity to enter into such an experience and have no inhibitions about 'talking cures' and the culture of counselling or therapeutic ideas.

Recent initiatives to expand the role of nurses and practitioners contribute to a blurring of roles often approved of by clients (Snelgrove and Hughes, 2000; Williams et al., 1999; Pearce, 1999). The stigma of child and adolescent mental health deters many young people from gaining access to the right help at the right time. This, combined with the profound feelings of guilt experienced by parents, which prevents them seeking support, means there is enormous unmet need in the community.

Innovative ways of responding to this need are required. Family support offers one way of bridging the gap between primary care responses and specialist family therapy input and the opportunity to engage with families who feel excluded from helping services. Bringing together different professionals in offering a more accessible, appropriate, and acceptable service for troubled young people and their families is a timely response to a growing problem. Family support services can intervene early over a short period of time, with an eclectic mix of practical and therapeutic activity. Professional rivalry and competitive fears of greater efficacy and role-blurring are challenged by evidence that paradoxically, the encouragement of generic interprofessional working actually reinforces boundaries between professions (Brown et al., 2000).

As family therapy continues to mature into a distinctive profession it is possible to see the mirroring of this phenomenon with teams of family therapists coming together from diverse professional backgrounds, while retaining their former values and knowledge base. There may be a degree of ambivalence about transforming from one professional role to another, with both advantages and disadvantages in maintaining a position of uncertainty.

This is as true for staff moving from family support to family therapy, or the other way round. Experienced family support staff are able to integrate in family therapy teams as they share a common skills base and theoretical assumptions. While practitioners who have qualified after extensive training to become family therapists and who are unable to secure a designated therapist post within a service, can work successfully in a family support service.

The multi-disciplinary nature of many family support staff groups or like-minded staff from different agencies can offer short-term intensive input, advice and information. Combined with parental guidance and direct work with children in their own homes or in preferred contexts such as schools, they can provide a non-stigmatising acceptable service. Parents gain motivation, want help and support, and listen to, and act upon, advice. This contrasts with the often negative and antagonistic relationship with statutory services working within child protection contexts.

In child and adolescent mental health services, non-urgent referrals have to join waiting lists to see family therapists. This prolongs family stress, amplifies symptomatology, and hampers engagement with the therapist, when the family are eventually offered an appointment. The clinic base, with its medical influence and often psychiatric leadership, can deter referrers and families from properly engaging with help due to the stigma of mental illness associated with such resources. Their remoteness and detachment from their communities make them intrinsically inaccessible and especially disconnected from socially excluded groups.

Conventional provision is unable to cope with demand, and yet is not being utilised by many of the most needy groups in society. Family support amongst other things seems to be offering a way into helping networks for families and children traditionally difficult to engage in work. The *Just Therapy* approach in New Zealand offers an example of proactive community involvement and a socio-political dimension for practice focussing on family strengths within a collaborative model of care.

Evaluations of social programmes aimed at addressing structural disadvantage in the US, or what has become known in the United Kingdom as **social exclusion**, suggest that a combination of intensive therapeutic intervention with policies designed to change social conditions, is required. Also, there is a need to find out more about how families cope without therapy or support. More families manage to find ways to overcome difficulties, than require help. It is something that occurs spontaneously within and between kinship, non-biological, and same-sex relationships all the time. Further research is required to investigate what families do right, how they succeed, and learn to manage change so that practitioners can learn from them.

Family therapists have much to learn from families and from family support staff, without restricting themselves to expert roles as supervisors or consultants. Family support staff can equally learn much from therapists trained to high standards with focussed theoretical parameters, and ethical and regulatory protection. Family therapists gain by positioning themselves within communities, in tune with economic and cultural experiences by more explicit acknowledgement of the social aspects to people's lives. Family support staff gain by adding to their repertoire of skills and knowledge, collaborating in more efficient and effective ways, and sharing best practice ideas. The answer to the question, whether the chicken came before the egg, may not be as important as to the one, why did the chicken cross the road? If it was to see what was on the other side, then family support and family therapy might like to cross the road.

CHAPTER 2

Family Systems Theory: Core Concepts

Introduction

Most individuals have 'significant others' with whom they relate. Thus, the skills of working with two or more people are vital to all those in the caring professions. An intervention with one person will affect their significant others and we need to be cognisant of this. As practitioners we should work with people in their family and community or ecological contexts. The skills of working with two or more people are best described and developed in the introductory texts in family therapy literature (Haley, 1991; Barker, 1998; Dallos and Draper, 2000). Once these are incorporated into our ways of working they can be utilised in many and varied situations. The skills of family therapy are readily transferable and relevant to all age groups.

The popularity of family therapy arose from its apparent effectiveness in enabling rapid change for families experiencing problems. One of the reasons for this appears to be the active inclusion of all family members in the process of change (Barker, 1998; Barnes, 1998), thereby avoiding situations where people feel excluded from what is happening to those they are close to or where they are resentful of change. The experience of feeling excluded can occur in many settings. A recent example encountered was at an application to renew a mental health section order for a young man of 20 years. His mother was struggling to understand the interventions and treatment plan for her son and described herself as feeling 'completely shut out'. In terms of his individual care the plans and treatment strategy were clear and appropriate. Working with the whole family, as well as the detained patient, would have enabled them to both understand and support the interventions rather than, as was beginning to happen, to begin to resist and undermine the strategy.

However it is not easy to get families together, and many workers do not feel comfortable dealing with the complexities of working with the family system. We would argue that for all professionals in the 'human' professions some of these skills are essential since the people who live together and relate together are in the best position to alter the circumstances for each other and to promote positive change. The reason that people come to need interventions is that they have encountered difficulty in dealing with a particular set of circumstances and need help to move on and to re-establish their family system using the strengths within the family.

There are many excellent introductory texts to family therapy (e.g. Barker, 1998; Dallos and Draper, 2000). Rather than try to repeat what is already written, we propose here to describe the core concepts and considerations for working with a family and then link these to family therapy practice. All family therapy is predicated on working with the family as a system and therefore we will look briefly at the key components of systems theory as relevant to family therapy and your work. We will also describe the importance of convening and engaging with a family and the issues of the life cycle and multicultural aspects as we feel these are crucial to the setting up of work with a family. How the process begins and what work is done even before seeing a family, are critical to the potential success of any intervention. People do not seek the help of professionals lightly, and our preparation for working with a family is crucial, and also easily rushed in busy professional practice.

Systems theory

Thinking of families as living systems with all the dynamics that this implies was quite revolutionary.

> Family therapy . . . looks at problems within the systems of relationships in which they occur, and aims to promote change by intervening in the broader system rather than in the individual alone.
> (Burnham, 1986: 2).

Systems theory enables professionals to think about how the family dynamics are constantly altering as each family member deals with life both inside and outside the family. This also introduces the ideas of family boundaries and the permeability of such boundaries. It moves thinking away from **linear causality** and introduces the idea of **circular causality**; that is, that change impacts and reverberates around the system in often unpredictable ways. The systemic ideas were readily embraced as helping to understand how the pieces of the family puzzle fit together. What do we mean by unpredictable results of change? Let us consider the 'A' family:

'A' Family

Mother, father and their two children, boys aged eight and five, live together. The parents are having difficulty with the elder boy's behaviour. Family work is undertaken which results in clearer rules for the boy's behaviour and with father spending more time with the elder boy. The elder boy's behaviour improves and everyone is happy until they notice that the younger boy's behaviour has deteriorated.

What has happened? The improvement in one problem area has led to another problem developing. This is not uncommon when working with families and the use of systems theory helps us to consider and anticipate some of the possible dynamics of change; the impact of change on all parts of the system needs to be considered. In social work practice when a child is removed from a family it is not unusual to find that another child takes on the role of the child who has been removed and the problems begin again. In other words dealing directly, or only, with the problem presented can lead to another issue developing and the use of systems theory can help prevent **symptom replacement**.

Systems theory originates in cybernetics (Von Bertalanffy, 1968). The ideas have been applied to family systems, and the key points which we need to think about and incorporate into our practice are:

- The parts of the family are interrelated.
- One part of the family cannot be understood in isolation from the rest of the system.
- Family functioning cannot be fully understood by simply understanding each of the parts.
- A family's structure and organisation are important factors determining the behaviour of family members.

Let us consider each of these briefly. That the parts of the family are interrelated is self evident but useful to revisit. In all practice there are times when there can be a preoccupation with one or two family members and the others can be marginalised. I would suggest that in family 'A' the younger child's needs were not given enough priority when designing an intervention targeted to try and improve the elder child's behaviour. This can easily happen even with experienced practitioners and so it is useful to revisit the interrelatedness of the family members.

These four points make the case for considering families systemically. In relation to your practice the second and third are of particular note. It is still not uncommon in practice to try to piece together the family's story by accessing or understanding parts of the family. The notion that this does not enable an understanding of the w   h   o   l   e   , if true, throws into question much of practice where family members are not seen together and some may not be involved at all. So if we cannot understand, lets say, a child in isolation from their family (point 2) and if we cannot understand the family by simply interviewing members separately (point 3) then the task of convening the family members relevant to the system under consideration needs to be undertaken.

It is easy to state this and even if apparently true many professionals working in the human services feel more comfortable interviewing people individually and believe that this enables people to speak more freely. The problem with this is that they are not communicating with the relevant family members and the worker/therapist becomes the holder of all information and the one who decides what is relevant for other family members to know. This is a very powerful position and not compatible with the ideas of working in partnership with users and carers. Also as individuals we all have our own slant or interpretation of the facts and it is more effective to share these in a family meeting with the relevant systems worker who can also provide a reality check.

The family structure and organisation (point 4) determine to some degree what is possible within a particular family. There is no 'normal' family structure. The question is, does this structure work for this family? Does it allow healthy growth for family members? This is where issues such as permeability of boundaries can be explored. Each system has a boundary and systems also contain subsystems and are located within suprasystems. In family terms there are subsystems within the family which have their own boundaries. Examples of the possible subsystems are parental, marital or sibling. There can also be grandparent subsystems and the existence of a suitable hierarchy between the generation is thought to be important (Hayley, 1991). The suprasystems to which the family may belong concern the extended family, community and other ecological groupings. If a family's boundaries are relatively impervious they may be isolated from their community and may be enmeshed in their relationships within the family. If a family's boundaries are too permeable the individuals in

the family may be disengaged from each other and overinvolved with the wider community. Enmeshment and disengagement were first described by Minuchin (1974).

Perhaps the 'B' Family will help us think more about structures and subsystems:

'B' Family

Mother, father and their two children, boys aged eight and five, live together with their maternal grandmother. The parents are having difficulty with the elder boy's behaviour and the referral suggests that they are being undermined by interference from Grandma.

With the 'B' family it could be argued that the parenting subsystem contains mother, father and grandmother. It may be that in relation to the family structure the task for therapy would then be to redefine these boundaries so that the parenting system becomes mother and father. In systems terms though, we will need to pay attention to the impact that this has on grandmother, who may not relinquish her parental role willingly, if addressed in terms of the structure this may lead to another problem developing. Each reader may like to pause here to consider their own position in relation to the merits and place for working with family systems.

Given that we are going to consider the family as a system what are the core considerations for facilitating this? What or who is the family? Who do we wish to convene? How are we going to engage with them? What stage of the life cycle are the family at and what is their family culture? These elements will set the scene for the first interview with the family where some of these issues will arise along with the problems that have brought the family to therapy.

Convening the family

Who should be convened for a family meeting at the beginning of work with the family? The purpose of the meeting will be to engage with the family and understand the reasons for referral before possibly undertaking a family assessment and deciding, with the family, on appropriate interventions which could be family, individual or some combination of both. The rationale for convening the whole family is that it is easier to understand the systemic nature of the problem from this starting point. And it is more difficult to get family members to attend later if they are needed than to begin together. Finally the therapist is less likely to be influenced by the views of the people who do attend which may be against those who are not there. (This last point takes us back to the difficulty of understanding the family through simply understanding each of the parts of it as discussed above.)

The first consideration here is the question of 'Who is the family?' that may be affected by the purpose of the interview. In other words is it all the people living in the household or just some of them? Should it include people beyond the family home? At first glance this seems rather a simple question. Considering the 'B' family again:

'B' Family

Mother, father and their two children, boys aged eight and five, live together with their maternal grandmother. The parents are having difficulty with the elder boy's behaviour and the referral suggests that they are being undermined by interference from Grandma.

One possibility is to invite all those living in the household and to use the opportunity to observe the whole system and hear everyone's view of the problem. Another approach would be to invite the parents and children and exclude the grandmother on the grounds that the family need to be recognised as a unit and given the opportunity to re-establish the boundary between themselves and the grandmother. Grandma could then be invited in at a later time if appropriate.

A different situation arises with the 'C' Family:

'C' Family

Mother, father and their two children, boys aged eight and five live together. After school the boys are looked after by their maternal grandmother, who lives nearby. The parents are having difficulty with the elder boy's behaviour.

This is a very similar scenario to the 'B' family. Here we could invite the family household and invite Grandma later, if this is indicated, or we could invite Grandma to the first interview, even though she does not live with the family to acknowledge her caretaking role and gather information about the child's behaviour in the two situations.

It can be seen from these two scenarios that the decision as to what constitutes the family system and therefore who to invite to the first interview will set the scene for the process of the therapy. The family system is therefore not necessarily easy to define and is located within the wider family and community systems.

Engaging with the family

Part of the process of convening the family involves engaging with each family member. Engaging occurs both during the convening and at the first interview. Having got the family to the first interview it is vital that all family members have the opportunity to engage with the therapist. Contact must be made with each individual, particularly if there has been contact with some members of the family already. For example in the 'B' family above if the practitioner has been in contact with the mother to organise the first meeting or to explain the reasons for wanting to see the whole family then they will need to engage with the father at the first interview. If it seems that there is already an alliance with mother it is easy for father to feel excluded and to allow mother to dominate the interview which compounds the situation. Similarly the children and grandmother, if she is invited, need to experience that their presence is valued or it will be hard to get them to return and engage with the process of change.

If a family member does not attend the interview the therapist may need to engage with them individually before inviting them to attend a future session. This is because having engaged with the rest of the family the member who did not attend will feel excluded and may be wondering what was said about them in their absence. This contact may be by letter, by telephone or through personal contact. Having thought about the family system, convened the family and engaged with the members there are other considerations which are relevant to all families and can be thought about during this initial contact phase. These would include the family **life cycle stage** and cultural aspects of family life.

Transitional challenges

Why is the life cycle so important? It identifies the tasks that the family have to deal with at the particular stage of life in which they are. Each stage has different developmental tasks for the family members. Being a couple requires quite different adaptations to being a couple with a baby. The needs and tasks faced by a family with young children are very different to those faced by a family with older children in the process of leaving home and so on. So looking at the family life cycle gives a window into the developmental needs of the individuals within the family. If these are not being met then they are likely to experience problems (Brown and Christensen, 1999; Dryden, 1988).

Again much is written about family development, particularly the family life cycle and we include only a brief summary here. Essentially then, the family life cycle tends to be thought of as a series of stages each with its own developmental task. The stage of the life cycle which the family are at will have relevance to understanding why they are experiencing difficulties at that particular point in time.

It has been widely proposed that families may experience problems at transition points in the life cycle (see Carter and McGoldrick, 1999, for full descriptions of the transition stages). It is thus important to be aware of the main transitions and some of the disruptions to these. A key factor in this view is that many families function well or at least do not perceive themselves as having problems for long periods of time. There must therefore be something specific which triggers the difficulties by creating circumstances which produce stress that the family are unable to negotiate. Many family therapists believe that moving from one stage of the life cycle to another can produce just such stress (Hoffman, 1981; Madanes, 1981). Examples of this are adjusting to the arrival of another child or a child entering adolescence. Each of the stages involves change for the family routines and there is also an emotional process of transition required.

The main stages of the life cycle which have been identified are shown in Table 2.1. Within these stages are many substages, and perhaps more importantly, families do not proceed neatly through the stages. We might expect adolescents to be leaving home around the time that grandparents are requiring more care when the family has spare capacity to deal with this. However, often grandparents become ill when children are still dependent and there is a conflict of interest and a heavy workload to negotiate. Similarly as the family enters the stage of 'The family with adolescents' another baby may arrive necessitating the family to negotiate two developmental stages at once.

Increasingly there are families where divorce or remarriage have taken place and this adds a different set of issues to the life-cycle stages that have to be negotiated. These may involve the loss of a natural parent and gain of a step-child, parent or grandparent. It will also involve negotiations between different family systems. These extensive

Table 2.1: Basic family life cycle

Family life cycle stage	Emotional process of transition
1. Between families: The unattached young adult	Accepting parent offspring separation
2. The newly married couple	Commitment to the new system
3. The family with young children	Accepting new members into the system
4. The family with adolescents	Increasing flexibility of family boundaries to include children's independence
5. Launching children and moving on	Accepting exits from and entries to the family system
6. The family in later life	Accepting the shift of generational roles

family arrangements inevitably involve complex family life cycle stages. Often the new couple will want to have children together as well as the children they already have. This increases the possibility of being a family with young children and also older children who may live elsewhere for all or part of the time requiring complex adaptations.

There are numerous possibilities concerning the life cycle which need your consideration and awareness and which may be key to the presenting problem. In the example of the arrival of a new baby in a family with adolescents, it is often expected that the adolescent is old enough to understand the intense physical demands of a baby. This may be the case at one level but almost invariably the adolescent experiences mixed emotions about the arrival of the baby and may find the decrease in attention towards themselves difficult to cope with. In families presenting at this stage these issues should be appraised.

Changes in life cycle stage can be difficult for many reasons including for example, anxiety about letting go in adolescence and adjusting to altered responsibilities with new arrivals in the family. In the intensity of dealing with a whole family interview we can lose sight of the life cycle issues which often offer simple explanations which make sense to the family.

Prior to the first meeting the practitioner should consider what the life cycle stage of the family is. They should consider what the life cycle issues and transitions appear to be for the family and prepare to confirm or moderate these during their assessment of the presenting problems and of family functioning. Sometimes the life cycle transition can be the key to the whole therapeutic process so it is a very important feature of any preparation for an initial assessment of a family.

Multi-cultural aspects

McGoldrick, Pearce and Giordano (1982) were among the first to draw attention to culture and ethnicity as crucial influences on the interactional style and structure of families. They also highlighted the importance of giving attention to ethnic groups within what is typically referred to as the majority culture.

In order to train multi-culturally sensitive therapists, the understanding of one's own ethnic and cultural background enables the student to have a context within which to understand the culture of others. It is important to appreciate that within the majority culture there is not a homogenous group (Preli and Bernard, 1993; Muncie et al., 1997). You need to be aware of the subtleties of their own ethnic and cultural make-up since multi-cultural therapy applies to both majority and minority cultures. The point here being that we cannot make assumptions about the internal structure of a family from their known culture since there is always individual interpretation in any culture or religion and we need to take the time to understand this.

Pursuing these ideas further Berg and Jaya (1993) looked at Asian-American families. They explored the concept of family uniqueness and started from the understanding that Asian-American families are like all other families, like some other families and like no other families. They believe that cultural sensitivity can be learned, and they looked at some culturally important values for this group. What follows are some generalisations so we must always remember that each family is unique and requires an individual approach. The need for careful assessment before any intervention is made is vital.

Family culture I

There is a long tradition in Asian culture of solving problems through mediation rather than through head-on confrontation. Berg and Jaya feel that family therapists are in a good position to mediate within a family's conflict because of their position of authority, knowledge of family relationships and techniques that enhance face saving with Asian families.

In this situation meeting with family members separately is suggested since airing their difficulties together at the outset may be too confrontative. This is in contrast to the suggestion we were making above of the importance of beginning family therapy with whole families. It highlights how every family situation needs individual appraisal by the therapists on receiving referrals to assess whether standard procedures, whatever they are in a particular agency, are appropriate for the particular family referred. The task of convening and engaging with the family will therefore vary though it will remain that the case that simply understanding the parts of the family will not enable an understanding of the whole family and the individual contact will need to be preparing the family for a family meeting. Berg and Jaya also give a salutary example of how the different cultures approach the same problem, using the example of behaviour control.

Family culture 2

American children who misbehave are often 'grounded'. Their punishment is to be forced to be with their family and it seems that one of the results of grounding is that American children fight their way out of the family (a process Americans call emancipation). With Asian children, being excluded from the family is extremely rare and is a severe punishment. Thus if children misbehave they are threatened with banishment from the family and told to get out. The children have to fight to stay in the family and the expectation is that children will remain within the family bringing their spouses to join it.

The point here is that neither approach is better or worse, simply that they are different and need to be understood before trying to intervene. An intervention based on the wrong premise for 'grounding' would otherwise totally fail and the therapist would be perplexed by this if they have assumed majority culture norms. In fact with any family these expectations should be checked.

The McMaster Models approach (Miller et al., 2000) of careful, systematic assessment of how a family organises itself in relation to the necessary tasks of family life is particularly appropriate for understanding the uniqueness of any family (see Chapter 4). It enables the therapist to spend a number of sessions with the family, in a structured way exploring their interaction patterns before embarking on 'treatment' ideas and strategies aimed at change. It is also a model which focuses on the therapist role as a facilitator, working in partnership with the family, enabling or empowering the family rather than instructing or directing them.

Messent (1992) working with Bangladeshi families in East London also points to the appropriateness of family therapy with Asian families because of the importance of interconnections between different family members, while urging caution on the techniques used. Structural techniques are considered appropriate but unbalancing the family should be avoided as this approach may be too confrontative.

Is it necessary or even desirable for practitioners to come from the same religious or cultural background? Different difficulties can arise in the situation of same culture, particularly where this is not the majority culture and issues around integration with the majority culture arise. Toledano (1996) writes of an issue that may arise in family therapy when the family and the therapist do come from the same religion or culture (in this case Judaism) and when the culture is a minority in society.

Family culture 3

The experience of a Jewish therapist working with Jewish families in an agency set up by 'Jewish Care' is that the families assume that he will support their interpretation of religious and cultural conflict, particularly in relation to intermarriage.

'How can therapists use their own experience and knowledge of their shared culture without imposing it on the family? A position of "not knowing" is helpful when the therapist operates almost as a curious anthropologist studying an unfamiliar culture. It is however problematic when the therapist is known to share the client's culture.' (Toledano, 1996: 293). This is helpful as it emphasises difference within groups and the difficulties that can arise when the assumption is of shared values and the expectation is that the therapist will support the same. It is not necessary to have the answers to a cultural or religious dilemma within a family but it is necessary to facilitate the process of the family in coming to a resolution of the dilemma.

An awareness and preparedness by the therapist to question their own and the families' position with respect to cultural and religious issues is essential. All authors stress the need for appreciation of uniqueness within any grouping.

Contra-indications for family therapy

There may be situations where family therapy is not a good idea. There is no general agreement as to a specific set of situations where family therapy is contra-indicated, but family therapy is not a panacea and its appropriateness for the problems referred should be evaluated. Listed below are four examples of situations where family therapy may not be appropriate:

- Where geographical distances make it impractical to convene the family.

- During child protection investigation and assessment.
- At times the family can present at too late a stage. This is often the case when the family have already decided to break up by the time they reach therapy. There will be things that can usefully be addressed together but the possibilities for change will be limited.
- Where a family member is already engaged in an individual treatment programme. Here family support may be indicated in order that the family are engaged in, and part of, the process but not necessarily in therapy as a family.

CHAPTER 3

Contemporary Methods and Models of Family Therapy

Introduction

Working with families – whatever the focus of assessment or intervention – probably forms the bedrock of modern practice, whether in elderly care, youth work community care, child care or mental health care. It is little wonder then that family therapy has always had enormous attraction for practitioners who want to help and support individuals and families in thoughtful and effective ways. Despite contemporary service provision being systematically defined in narrow case/care management terms, there are many opportunities inside and outside statutory and voluntary services for using some of the skills and techniques associated with systems theory to aid assessment and intervention practice.

The added bonus is that individuals, couples and families consistently report satisfaction with the approach (Carr, 2000). Nevertheless, many staff feel ambivalent or at least apprehensive about using therapeutic techniques, especially as there are institutional constraints that magnify their personal reservations. At best this is because practitioners do not wish to do any harm, or because they fear unleashing psychological forces within the family that they feel responsible for. These are understandable concerns that need to be put in perspective against the reliable evidence and testimony of practitioners and service users who can confirm positive experiences. The full range of practice models and methods employed by caring staff can be subject to the same doubts,

yet this does not prevent practitioners using task centred or crisis intervention techniques for example. Some practitioners feel they should be fully qualified family therapists or at least in training before trying to use systems theory and skills. Yet practitioners do not have to be fully qualified psychotherapists to use psychodynamic skills, or psychologists to use cognitive-behavioural methods which are part of everyday practice for many. It is also the case that seemingly functional or administrative procedures without any ostensible therapeutic intent can stimulate unexpected behaviour or emotional reactions in service users consistent with a therapeutic effect.

In the same way, practitioners can quite properly use the skills and techniques of family therapy as part of their broad repertoire of applied theories to bring to bear on the challenges presented to them by people in need. The advantages outweigh the disadvantages as we shall see, particularly as the model of family therapy was envisaged as a short term intervention in contrast to the traditional long term individual casework relationship identified with some practice. Even small pieces of work can make a big difference, and the most intractable of situations can be transformed by the application of systems theory. Indeed the application of systems theory may not need to be within the family but instead directed at the wider professional system where a bigger problem may reside that is negatively impacting on the service users. We shall look more closely in Chapter 9 at research evidence into the evaluation and effectiveness of family therapy where it is practised in a range of contexts, in order to assess its suitability for use by practitioners.

For now, we review some of the important developments in systems theory and examine some of the more popular and accessible methods and models of family therapy and challenge the notion that practitioners do not have the time, training or appropriate context to employ them. There are challenges in using systems theory in certain statutory settings especially where the bureaucratic structures require families to acquire labels such as 'in need' or to conform to child protection terminology. These professional systems do not lend themselves to empowering therapeutic working methods even though they have the potential for being experienced as more helpful and more cost-effective in the long term.

And just as you would explain the aims and intentions of your work using any other method of intervention, so it is the same for employing a family therapy approach. If you are trying to work in partnership and offering a degree of choice in the way you can help it is probably an advantage in being able to explain the rationale behind your practice approaches. Naturally, for those who are reluctant and resentful clients this may feel like a false exercise. But if you persevere and have a preference about this way of working, then the process of an open and honest discussion can set the framework for engaging service users and signal a respectful attitude.

Historical context

Modern family therapy as we understand it is generally credited with emerging in the 1950s as a result of a number of developments in the fields of psychology, communication theory, and psychiatry. At a broader level it is also important to acknowledge the socio-economic context of post second world war economic expansion, population growth, and the significance of cultural changes affecting people's attitudes to sex, marriage, leisure and intimate relationships. The 1950s in the developed industrialised countries were therefore a time of rapid sociological change

and economic growth, when new ideas were more easily articulated and received.

One of the important factors that stimulated the embryonic ideas that were to grow into a new form of psycho-therapy was a growing dissatisfaction with the traditional psycho-analytic model of individual therapy. This was combined with new research that demonstrated effectiveness when groups of people were brought together to talk about their problems. Two key figures stand out as influential at this time in moving forward the ideas that were to crystallise in the practice of family therapy. Ludwig von Bertalanffy (1968) was a German biologist who devised a general systems theory that could be used to explain how an organism worked by studying the transactional processes happening between different parts. He understood that the whole was greater than the sum of its parts and that we could observe patterns and the way relationships were organised in any living system.

Gregory Bateson (1973) and others in the USA took this concept of a general systems theory and combined it with the new science of cybernetics and applied it to social systems such as the family. Cybernetics had introduced the idea of information processing and the role of feedback mechanisms in regulating mechanical systems. Bateson used this notion to argue that families were systems involving rules of communication and the regulatory function of feedback that influenced patterns of behaviour within them. In the UK, Ronald Laing (1969) challenged the orthodoxy in psychiatric practice by arguing that schizophrenia was a product of family dysfunction, while John Bowlby (1969) moved from treating individuals to treating families where an individual was displaying mental health problems.

The idea began to take root therefore that individual experiences within families were continually being shaped and influenced by the evolving interaction of patterns of communication. Individuals were not therefore determined by early traumatic experiences or distorted developmental transitions, as the prevailing therapeutic orthodoxy argued. Family therapy thinking conceptualised that individual personality and identity could change along with changes in family dynamics. From this common root and systemic theory a number of models and methods of family therapy practice evolved through to the present day. The following have been selected to illustrate the range of more common approaches and their usefulness to practitioners.

Structural family therapy

Structural family therapy is a therapy of **action**. The tool of this therapy is to modify the present, not to explore and interpret the past. Since the past was instrumental in the creation of the family's present organisation and functioning, it is manifest in the present and will be available to change by interventions that change the present (Minuchin, 1974).

The structural family therapist engages with the family system and then sets out to transform it. The main focus of this approach is the family structure with the underlying assumption that the problematic behaviour is related to a fault with the functional normative family structure. Structural family therapists believe that by changing the family structure they can change the position of family members and therefore alter their subjective experiences.

The process of the model is that changes to the structure of the family create the possibility for further change. The notion that the family system is organised around the support, regulation, nurturance and socialisation of its members means that the therapist needs to repair or modify the family's functioning so that it can better perform these tasks. Once a change has been introduced the family will therefore preserve that change by the family's own self-regulating mechanisms. Changes in the multiple interactions between family members will lead to the possibility of change in the experience of the individual.

The characteristics of structural family therapy stem from the classic systemic technique of observing the interactive patterns in a family. Once this baseline of behaviour can be understood as contributing to the problem a structural approach would seek to highlight these, interrupt them when they are happening, and then get the family to re-enact them in different ways that lead to different outcomes. The attraction to practi-

tioners in this way of using family therapy techniques is that it aspires to provide families with **problem-solving practical solutions**. In a family session therefore the task is to enable the family to try out different ways of doing things, for example by coaching a parent on how to maintain a boundary or limit the behaviour of their child.

Practitioners who are attracted to behavioural approaches to their practice will find certain similarities with structural family therapy in that learning is practical, enabling family members to observe their own changes. These are some of the key features (Gorell-Barnes, 1984):

Intensity: creating a much focussed experience of emotionally charged interaction rather than skipping over uncomfortable feelings.

Persistence: concentrating on these long enough to make a difference to the problem patterns brought to your attention.

Homework: taking home tasks which transfer what has been learnt to the home context. This assists the momentum of change.

Confirmation: seeing the positive connotations of behaviour and emphasising people's competence is necessary to challenging negative, fixed ideas.

Enactment: involves requesting a family to move from description to actually showing the problem live in the session. Encouraging people to talk directly to each other rather than through the medium of the practitioner.

Changing space: this literally involves moving people around in the session. It is especially powerful when a child is being caught in the crossfire between fighting parents, or used as a go-between. Asking the parents to sit and face each other can be simple yet incredibly transformational.

Creating boundaries: applicable in situations where age-appropriateness and enmeshment are issues. For example, where there is poor individuation it helps family members separate themselves. It can be of value where parents experience small children as tyrannical and out of control, or where adolescents are finding independence difficult.

Strategic family therapy

One of the guiding principles in **strategic family therapy** is that problems apparently residing in one individual are frequently associated with the difficulties resulting from a family's need to change and reorganise at transitional stages. These can occur at times such as the birth of a baby or when a young person is considering leaving home (Dallos and Draper, 2000). This is particularly the case with older adolescents who present with mental health problems or a history of school refusal. This can indicate a family dynamic whereby the young person becomes symptomatic in order to help parents avoid conflict in their relationship. Thus attention is focussed on the young person rather than the parents.

One of the central premises of the strategic approach is that people are essentially strategic in the way that they are involved in predicting how others may think, feel and act. Some writers characterise this as indicative of a constant power struggle in which family members are trying to influence each other and define themselves (Haley, 1976). Furthermore this struggle is not confined within the family but also occurs when the family seek help. In everyday practice various family members will seek to influence the practitioner and try to gain sympathy or agreement with their particular perception of the problem.

The implication for your practice is that you can use this approach starting from the basis that parents for example, will seek to enlist you to their side in a struggle with an unruly adolescent. Colluding with this will only distance you from the adolescent and diminish your effectiveness in resolving the problems between parents and child. The strategic approach recognises explicitly the dilemmas presented by families who seek help but want to remain in control. These beliefs and premises highlight the role played by attempted solutions to problems which either make matters worse or result in denial of the seriousness of the problem.

The strategic approach, in contrast to the structural approach, does not have a normative concept of the family that should exist according to set hierarchies and sub-systems of parents/children etc. Rather the focus with strategic family therapists is on the day-to-day interactions which have resulted in problems, and the cognitive thinking being applied to solve them. The perceptions people have about these problems invariably influences how they try to tackle them. Attempted solutions and behavioural responses that actually maintain the problem require challenging and shifting with alternatives promoted by the therapist. These are some of the key features of strategic family therapy (Dallos and Draper, 2000):

Staged approach: detailed exploration of the difficulties to be resolved is translated into an **action plan** designed to disrupt embedded problematic sequences. Assessment and reappraisal of the outcomes of intervention is used to revise or continue tasks.

Directive tasks: these usually consist of homework that family members are asked to carry out between family sessions. They are most effective when every family member is involved in such tasks. The aim is to alter problematic sequences of interactions. The important point is that the task must be reasonable and fit within the family's repertoire of achievable limits.

Paradoxical tasks: this is where the family are asked to do the opposite of what the therapist intends to happen. They are employed when families find it impossible to carry out directive tasks. The aim is to encourage symptomatic behaviour, in other words to try to unblock a cycle of failure and poor motivation and hopelessness. An example is where a family report constant bickering and loud arguments, describing family life as conflictual and uncaring. By suggesting that the family have one huge argument at a regular time each evening presents them with a double bind. If they do it, then they are demonstrating that they *can* control their behaviour and are therefore not helpless; if they do *not* do it because it feels stilted and manufactured, then they are learning not to argue. Either way change has occurred.

Milan systemic family therapy

The development of this model began in Italy in the 1970s where a group of psychiatrists were experimenting with treating individuals diagnosed as schizophrenic in a radically different way to the orthodox methods then employed. They reported better outcomes when they worked with the whole family rather than the individual patient. The central theoretical idea informing this approach is that the symptomatic behaviour of a family individual is part of the transactional pattern peculiar to the family system in which it occurs. Therefore the way to change the symptom is to change the rules of the family.

The goal of this therapy is to discover the current systemic rules and traditional myths which sustain the present dysfunctional patterns of relating, and to use the assumed resistance of the family towards outside help as a provocation to change. Change is achieved by clarifying the ambiguity in relationships that occur at a nodal point in the family's evolution. Milan systemic therapists do not work to a normative blueprint of how an ideal family should function (Burnham, 1986). This approach furthermore emphasises the importance of the underlying beliefs held by family members about the problem which affected behaviour. It avoids being perceived as blaming the non-symptomatic members of the family by working on the basis that the actions of various family members are the best they can do (Dallos and Draper, 2000). These are some of the key features:

Positive connotation: this technique is used as an extension of the strategic paradoxical task by reflecting back to the family a positive reason for all their actions. This is supported by providing a rationale for why they behave as they do, and maintains the therapist in a non-judgmental stance. It places the family members on an equal footing thus avoiding scapegoating.

Hypothesising: this is a way of bringing together all the available information prior to the family session and collating it into a coherent whole which is fully circular and systemic. In other words it attempts to explain why the family have a problem. This unproved supposition is tentative and is used as the basis for guiding the family session. The task for the therapist is to confirm or disprove the hypothesis and create a new one if necessary.

Circular questioning: this unique style of questioning is both elegant and simple. It requires the therapist to ask questions of one member about the relationship between two other family members. The family will not be used to communicating in this way and are placed in a position of having to speak freely about ideas they would normally keep to themselves. Differences in perception and distinctions in behaviour can be explored and discussed according to the interviewer's curiosity and hypothesis.

Neutrality: again, this is another distinguishing feature of systemic family therapy practice. It involves the therapist siding with everyone and showing no allegiance or favouritism to any individual family member. Although the therapist may feel distinctly biased towards say, a victim of abuse or domestic violence, the neutrality refers to behaviour during the interview. The aim is to maximise the family's engagement and not collude with blaming behaviour which will undermine the desired change.

The intervention: at the end of a family session a **prescription** or **intervention** is delivered to all those present and mailed to any absent members. It can consist of a paradoxical injunction, simple task or complex ritual designed to interrupt dysfunctional behavioural patterns (Campbell and Draper 1985).

Team working: this is not exclusive to Milan systemic family therapy but it is a particular characteristic of this method where the concept of live supervision during a family session is considered essential. The use of one-way screens, videos and audio-tapes are used to enable several people to bring their collective experience and knowledge to bear on the presented problems. This helps guard against the individual therapist being drawn into subtle alliances or missing important information during lively sessions. You can adapt this in your work context by having a colleague join you in some work and act as an observer to the process.

Brief solution-focussed therapy

As the title suggests this approach is primarily aimed at a short term period of work with the emphasis on encouraging families to recognise their own competencies. The mantra of practitioners using this way of working is 'focus on solutions not problems'. For example, a family or parents often discuss a child or a parent in sweeping generalisations when explaining their problems. 'He's always getting into trouble with teachers', or 'she never does as she is told'. These are recognisable complaints and express less the reality than an over-emphasis on the negative, as if the parents are trying to convince you of their case for help and their desperation. Solution-focussed therapists turn this idea around and carefully enable the complainants to recall an exception to this general rule about the trouble-some child (de Shazer, 1982; Berg, 1991).

Once the family has recognised that exceptions do occur and the person can behave or do as they are asked, the focus of the approach is to emphasise these exceptions and help the family to make more of them happen. This requires patience and systematic work to excavate every element surrounding these exceptions so that a family can prepare for them, recognise them, sustain them, and reproduce them. These are then translated into clear, recognisable goals that can be specifically described so that everyone involved can perceive them. Goal setting can often be difficult especially with parents or families who have poor self-esteem, are lacking in confidence, and feeling disempowered. To help overcome this difficulty the 'miracle question' is designed to help families identify specific behaviours and actions that indicate change, rather than talk abstractly about wanting to 'be happy again' or 'like a normal family'.

The miracle question entails asking the family to imagine that while they were all asleep a miracle happened and the problem was solved. When they awoke they were not aware that a miracle had happened. They then have to describe what is different that tells them a miracle has occurred. In describing the difference they are encouraged to make concrete the conditions for change and by doing so are in fact illustrating the goals they desire. The therapist's job is to work collaboratively with the families' own definition of change and help them devise ways of achieving it. Overall the brief solution-focussed approach can be summarised in terms of three rules (Dallos and Draper, 2000):

If it ain't broke don't fix it: even the most chronic of problems show periods where the troublesome patterns or symptoms are absent or reduced. The therapist needs to have a broad and tolerant view of what is not broke – what are competencies. These can be built upon so that therapy does not become bogged down into attempting to build a pursuit of a utopian family.

Once you know what works do more of it: once exceptions and competencies have been discovered then families are encouraged to do more of these. This can lead to a self-reinforcing cycle of success which will start to replace that of failure, incompetence and desperation.

If it doesn't work, don't do it again; do something different: families often become involved in cycles where they cannot see any alternative but to continue to act in the ways they always have, or do more of the same. While searching for the exception they can be helped to notice when an alternative pattern happens, occasionally with more positive consequences. This is built upon until it replaces the previous more common negative pattern.

Common characteristics of family therapy

Genograms/family trees: are a neat, cost-effective, and engaging way of introducing the family to a different type of practice. Used appropriately at the right time and in the right place they can help focus the whole family in a collaborative exercise that reveals a great deal of information in a non-threatening way. It is a way of addressing issues that are difficult to verbalise by physically drawing a picture or diagram of several generations of the family. Older family members as well as quite young children can join in. Deaths, divorces, separations, births and marriages can all be illustrated and committed to a large sheet of paper that can serve as a map of the family process for use in future sessions. Genograms can give families their first under-standing of intergenerational family relationship patterns. Sibling relationships can be described and discussed in a detached way without forcing a confrontation between two rivalrous young people or colluding with an exclusive and problematic closeness. The opportunity for the family themselves to generate hypotheses or

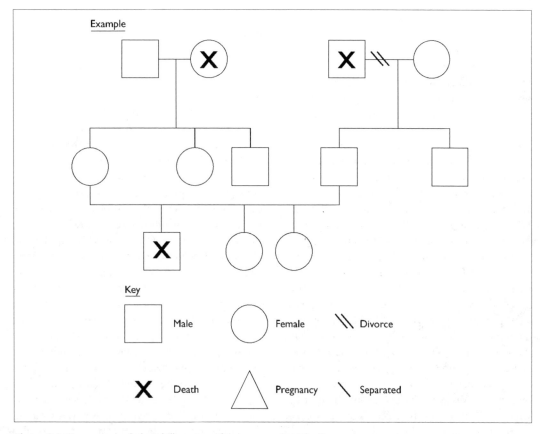

Figure 3.1: Genogram symbols and illustration of three-generational family

narratives to explain the impact of various events can be offered by a detailed and carefully constructed genogram. Beware the attraction of predicting pattern repetition though, as this may result in further individual scapegoating. The value in noting pattern is in the meaning this has for the family concerned (for example, are they actively resisting the repetition of early divorce or child care proceedings, or do they feel that their fate has already been sealed). Genograms are thus a relatively emotion-free way of collecting information that makes sense to the family and connects them to the therapeutic exploratory process (Goldenberg and Goldenberg 2004). Figure 3.1 shows some typical elements involved in constructing a family genogram.

Videos/one-way screens: are associated with the practice of family therapy and probably go some way to inhibit practitioners from getting involved. It can feel de-skilling to have your practice scrutinised so openly. The technology appears de-humanising and deceitful and it raises proper concerns about confidentiality and informed consent. However, in practice most families are not bothered by the use of videos or one-way screens/mirrors and their use is becoming more common in all kinds of non-statutory and family support settings. If these tools are properly explained and introduced to the participants as a means of helping the workers to be more effective, there are rarely objections. In many cases families can be encouraged to take video recordings home with them to review their own behaviour and learn how negative interactions are started and perpetuated. They can therefore be an additional learning resource and can make a point more powerfully than the verbal reasoning of even the most skilled therapist.

Supervision/joint working: is another characteristic of family therapy that distinguishes it from conventional managerial supervision that relies upon mainly verbal feedback from the supervisee. This form of supervision has a number of drawbacks that have been identified over the years including: information selectivity, the power differential between manager/worker, forgetfulness, focus on content rather than process, and differences in theoretical stance. Family therapy on the other hand has had a rare openness in relation to exposing practice to wider scrutiny, compared to individual-oriented therapies. Apart from the use of video recordings as a way of analysing the complex family patterns of interaction that are impossible to track during an interview, they can also be used as a training tool. Family therapy sessions are usually supervised live, involving at least another person observing the session and offering feedback and suggestions during the work or at a planned mid-point break. The person(s) observing are able to gain a different perspective to the worker involved with the family and spot important aspects that may benefit from a supportive suggestion. This notion has been developed to include the use of reflecting teams whereby the people behind the screen or mirror join the family and the worker in front to openly discuss their perceptions (Anderson, 1990).

Context of problems: is more than anything perhaps the most defining characteristic of family therapy practice. It means that whatever the problem being presented to you as a practitioner using systems theory you will automatically begin to ask a series of questions that are linked to the context of the presenting problem. This relates to not just the family context but the wider professional, public, socio-economic and cultural context of the problem. In other words it is an ecological approach in that it posits not just individuals as inter-linked within families but families as inter-linked in communities that are in turn inter-linked to class, ethnic groups, cultures etc, etc . . . It is a way of beginning the reframing process and looking at the problem from a different angle so that the concept of blame begins to be eroded and replaced with the concept of understanding the patterns that create and maintain the current problem. For example, one favourite question asked by many family therapists

at some point to each member of a family is, 'If this problem were to disappear what problem would be left to concern you?' This illustrates the different way of working compared to approaches that can unwittingly reinforce the family's dependence on a particular problem. Understanding the overall context of the problem offers another way of tackling it rather than seeking to change an individual or indeed trying to change a family.

Circularity/patterns: is again characteristic of whatever model of family therapy appeals to your style of work. It is a foundational assumption of all family therapists that problematic behaviour is conceived as forming part of a reflexive, circular motion of events and behaviours without beginning or end. Being able to spot the circular process and articulate it in a meaningful way with the family offers a positive way forward. This releases the therapist and the family to think beyond linear causality and blaming or scapegoating behaviour. The important distinction when using this conceptual framework is where abusive adults use grooming behaviour, and their power, to abuse children and young people. In these child protection cases and in domestic violence situations the motivation and responsibility need to be firmly located with the perpetrator. The circular understanding of problems offers an elegant explanatory tool for the reasons for the symptoms and other dysfunctional behaviour. Within a family any action by one member affects all other members and the family as a whole. Each member's response in turn prompts other responses that affect all other members, whose further reactions provoke still further responses etc. Such a reverberating effect in turn affects the first person, in a continuous series of chains of influence (Goldenberg and Goldenberg, 2004).

Case illustration

Having reviewed some of the more common methods and models of family therapy practice, it is important not to take these new concepts to a level of abstraction where they cease to be useful. It is easy to be seduced into the technocratic skills and mechanisms of therapeutic working at the expense of missing human responses in family members and yourself to what emerges during a family session. You may become an efficient therapist in terms of technical ability but are experienced as cold, distanced and emotionally unavailable. One way of guarding against this is to do some preparation before embarking on a piece of work by reflecting on your own family system. This includes early childhood memories which you may want to prompt with the use of photographs or familiar objects and places. Try constructing your own family genogram using the symbols and example in Table 3.1. Draw connections between other family members you feel close to or distanced from. Think about the family history going back several generations writing pen pictures of grandparents' relationships and characteristics, behaviours, and mannerisms etc. Recall those poignant stories or significant events that affected you and your family.

Commentary

This exercise should help you maintain contact with the real feelings and experiences generated when working at a therapeutic level with client families. Some practitioners will find this exercise too distressing or uncomfortable while others will find it enlightening and empowering. You may find it helpful to conduct the exercise jointly with a trusted colleague or friend, or even a family member. Be prepared for a powerful experience and anticipate the need to talk it through with someone afterwards – this might be a team leader or counsellor or a friend who is good at listening in a non-judgmental way. Knowing yourself is a pre-requisite for modern practice and is very much the case for working with families where you are engaging them at a deeper level. Understanding your own family heritage and the events and issues that have shaped all the individuals, offers you some personal insight as well as an idea of what it feels like to expose the past and explore its impact on the present. A thorough knowledge of your family process can help you avoid over-identifying with a similar family or help avoid persecuting a different family. Awareness of your own feelings of vulnerability and sensitive family issues can prepare you for negotiating these in a more sympathetic and thoughtful way with families you work with.

Contemporary developments

Convergent practice: this is characterised as the narrowing of the gap with some traditional psychodynamic theories that have informed individual therapeutic work. This is an interesting development in the sense that the evolution of family therapy has come full circle round to the original theoretical base it sprang from. Several contributors have discussed the previously unspoken notion of a combined or integrated family therapy practice that reflects and incorporates elements of psychodynamic therapy (Pocock, 1997; Larner, 2000; Donovan, 2003). This development demonstrates that systems theory is still a flexible, evolving paradigm within which approaches and techniques have remained fixed in some ways and changed in many others. This should suit practitioners who whilst interested in particular approaches to their work, nevertheless are agile enough to incorporate ideas and skills that can best help clients at particular times. Given the psychoanalytic root of modern psycho-social practice there is a valuable opportunity for practitioners to build on a solid theoretical foundation with skills and techniques that can feel relevant to many service users. An example is in the use of interpretation. This is one of the most powerful aspects of a psychodynamic approach that can be seen mirrored in the family therapy technique of a reflecting team conversation.

Feminist approaches: evolved more overtly during the 1980s as female family therapists began to discuss and write about power and gender relations within families (Perelberg and Miller, 1990; Goldner, 1991; Hare-Mustin, 1991). Their feminist analysis of therapeutic work revealed that couples were strongly influenced by assumptions about gender roles and expectations within relationships and families. Despite 30 years of feminist theory and practice in other contexts these writers and many female family therapists began to articulate a challenge to the gender-neutral concepts in orthodox family therapy theory and practice. Instead of assuming parity between partners or married couples they incorporated an understanding of the inequality conditioned and socialised into heterosexual relationships that explained domestic violence at one extreme, or at the other a stereotype of the passive or nurturing female and assertive or emotionally distant male.

Where problems occur in relationships they can often be better evaluated through a gendered lens that highlights the contradictions and dilemmas between people who are constrained by powerful concepts of maleness and femaleness. When people fail to conform to the societal norm of working man and child-caring female it is usually expressed as the female failing. Orthodox family therapists however well-intentioned would try to reverse the stereotype by seeking to engage the male partner in more child care duties but this in many cases simply reinforced the female's sense of failure. This attempted intervention neglected to understand that for many women success in child care was an important defining characteristic of their femininity from which they gained enormous self-esteem and role satisfaction. The intervention also unwittingly reinforced the male as the problem-solver and the more successful partner.

Practitioners using an empowering anti-oppressive framework to their practice will find these concepts resonate with their way of working with women who are abused by violent partners or left to cope with children on their own. Combining feminist family therapy concepts with caring skills you can overtly address the wider social context of the difficulties and dilemmas faced by women by challenging the prevailing patriarchal assumptions that undervalues child care and the relationship and nurturing skills of women. Helping women recover from such traumas and build self-confidence requires patience as well as the ability to reframe them away from notions of individual fault, blame, or failure towards an understanding of the social constraints affecting relationship patterns. Using a feminist approach means making explicit throughout your work with clients the power differences between genders and enabling them to tackle the consequent dilemmas in their relationships.

Constructivism and social constructionism: these two related but different concepts are linked to post-modern theories that have recently begun to challenge some of the orthodox thinking and techniques of family therapy practice. The post-modern thesis rejects the notion that there is a fixed truth or single reality about family process. The post-modern view suggests that each individual constructs his or her personalised views and interpretations of what the family might be experiencing together. Family therapists with a constructivist or social constructionist perspective emphasise the importance of cultural diversity, multiple realities and the acceptance of a wide range of belief systems (White and Epston, 1990; Goldenberg and Goldenberg, 2004). **Constructivism** stems from the study of the biology of cognition which argues that individuals have unique nervous systems that permit different assumptions being made about the same situation. **Social constructionism** is similar in that it argues that there is no such thing as objective reality, but that what we do construct from what we observe arises from the language system, relationships and culture we share with others. In practice the constructivist and social constructionist family therapist therefore would be recognised by their more collaborative style of working. The focus is on helping the family examine and reassess the assumptions individuals make about their lives rather than focussing on family patterns of communication. Using these approaches involves taking a position of uncertainty and not knowing; instead the therapist joins in the search for workable solutions on an equal basis with the family.

Narrative therapy: this recognises the natural ability people have to possess, to generate and to evolve new narratives and stories to make sense of their experiences (Freeman et al., 1997). The focus of interest is the meanings that families generate to explain and shape possible courses of actions. Traditions within families and cultures are used to guide interpretations of events. Making these more explicit in a more conversational style of therapeutic process helps to validate the family experience rather than seeking to impose a solution or follow a therapist-determined path. The nature of the conversation is the key to this approach. Practitioners will note similarities with an exchange model of assessment, empowering and service-user focussed work. The approach challenges the way clients are labelled because they are usually superficial, negative and one-dimensional descriptions. The client can begin to accept these limiting descriptions and believing they are 'true' and start to behave in ways that confirm the label. **Narrative therapy** aims to help families by collaborating in developing alternative stories about their lives and replacing a single, problem-saturated belief with a number of different, complex beliefs that open up possibilities.

Why practitioners might find family therapy useful

The attraction of family therapy for many practitioners using the techniques or pursuing advanced training to gain formal registration is no more or less than for any other method of practice. It will suit some while repel others. Practitioners interested in employing therapeutic work with families and recognising the limitations of working with individuals will find it offers a more comprehensive theoretical knowledge base that can incorporate both elements of the psychosocial paradigm. Family therapy immediately brings into the picture of information gathering and assessment, questions about the *context* of the presenting problem. This can appeal to practitioners who feel modern managerial approaches to practice ignore or discount the political, economic and social policy impact on family functioning.

It offers an explanatory tool and conceptual resource with which to give voice to people oppressed and victimised by a patriarchal capitalist system. On the other hand family therapy can offer the most psychodynamically oriented practitioner a theoretical and practical resource with which to explore the micro level of interpersonal transactions within and between kinship relationships that defy straightforward advice and support. Unique techniques such as those mentioned earlier can release bottled-up feelings and promote new conversations between partners or parents and children that were previously repressed or displaced. Self-defeating patterns of behaviour or dangerous acting out can be identified and understood in a different context than orthodox individual fault and blame explanations.

The advantage is that in family therapy everyone can be harnessed to tackle the problem(s) and with this collective investment everyone can be identified with a positive outcome. In child protection contexts a careful balance has to be struck between therapeutic potential and risk assessment. Joint working with another colleague or agency can help as can your capacity to wear two hats at once provided you have access to good quality supervision. Practitioners can therefore properly adopt a different position than that prescribed by the statutory role. By adopting a position of *not-knowing* the solution and committing yourself *with the family* to the search for a solution, you can be released from the burden of dual responsibility that can stymie practice manoeuvrability. This is particularly important in the contemporary context of the ethnically rich and culturally diverse society in which a myriad of different family forms, traditions, and beliefs exist. Thus family therapy offers practitioners a vehicle for adopting a partnership and empowering approach which maintains the family in the driving seat.

The challenge in taking on a therapeutic stance using systems theory is that it requires you to partly relinquish the often bureaucratic, formalised inspectorial role with all the dull paraphernalia of reports, meetings, procedures and legal requirements. These aspects of your role are exactly the opposite of what will engage families or parents struggling to survive on income support, in bad housing with poor health and a raft of emotional and behavioural problems. The negative image conveyed by the trappings of power and officialdom only serves to alienate and distance you from those desperate for help and a way out of their difficulties. By immersing yourself in the nitty-gritty of family life (who does what; what causes arguments; how do jobs get allocated; when do children go to bed; why is someone not going to school etc.) you and the family can explore new solutions and strategies. By tackling the small issues the family will be able to learn to think and act differently and in so doing be better equipped and more able to tackle the bigger issues confronting them.

CHAPTER 4

Assessment in Family Therapy

Introduction

Assessment with families is often taken for granted, sometimes the subject of unwarranted attention, but always a potentially liberating and empowering experience for you, the practitioner, and the service user. It is important that you understand how effective assessment takes into account people's needs, rights, strengths, responsibilities and resources. You need to reflect on how your individual practice enables you to identify clients' strengths rather than weaknesses, and work with their existing systems, networks and communities.

Organisational restrictions and resource constraints will militate against creative practice which is focussed on the service user, but you need to overcome these. Understanding how oppression and discrimination influences contemporary assessment practice and service users' ability to function is an important task for your practice development. Government guidance and the professional literature have begun to accept that assessment and intervention should be seamless parts of a continuous process. It also expects there to be a therapeutic dimension to this area of practice:

> The provision of appropriate services should not await the end of the assessment but be offered when they are required by the child and family. The process of engaging in an assessment should be therapeutic and perceived of as part of the range of services offered.
>
> (DoH, 2000).

However, employers tend to emphasise assessment skills to the detriment of good, integrated, holistic practice. The trend towards retrenchment in welfare services and reduction of work to bureaucratic care management for example is not meeting the needs of vulnerable service users who want more than administrative processing. Practitioners who cherish their core helping skills will find systems theory and family therapy practice both supports and extends their practice. Assessment underpinned by systems theory offers a useful tool to engage in holistic assessment practice rather than determining narrow eligibility criteria or negative risk assessment. Let us now think about the 'B' family from Chapter 2.

'B' Family

Mother, father and their two children, boys aged eight and five, live together with their maternal grandmother. The parents are having difficulty with the elder boy's behaviour and the referral suggests that they are being undermined by interference from Grandma.

With the information we have we could discuss the problem as the family see it and propose a parenting strategy which, in general terms might be expected to lead to improved behaviour management. The only problem with this approach is that we don't know what the reason is behind the fact that this is not already happening. It could be that there are some marital difficulties and mum is relying on grandma for emotional support. It could be that the child has some specific learning difficulties and is expressing frustration. There are many explanations, which could be imagined, and the question of whether or not to assess family functioning must be visited.

With the 'B' family in Chapter 2 we were thinking about who to invite to the initial meeting, how to engage the family, and about life cycle and cultural issues. Once we are engaged in a family meeting what are we going to do? Do we want to assess family functioning or do we want to hear the story and try an intervention based on the description of current concerns rather than underlying family processes? We know the outline of the problem; and the question, which we will address in this chapter, is how we could go about assessing family functioning. If we want to understand family processes we will need to use a model of family therapy to help us decide which areas of family life are important to understand. Examples of such areas might be **family roles** and **patterns of communication**.

Which model of family therapy?

There are a number of different family therapy models proposed as ways of understanding family processes. Each suggests ways to assess a family and they often take different starting points. Some suggest starting 'where the family is' with the problems presented. The presenting problem is a major motivating force for change and once tackled other problems may or may not emerge and the family may or may not wish to deal with them. Other models suggest careful, systematic assessment of the areas of family life deemed to be important to family functioning before intervening in the family. They propose that an intervention needs to be carefully designed to give the best opportunity for the family to experience success. Yet again other models suggest that if an intervention fails this gives information about the family and can be used to inform future interventions.

Clearly from the plethora of approaches a starting point has to be selected to develop the skills of assessing and working with families. Usually therapists select models which fit with their personal preference in terms of style of working. Do they prefer to let the story unfold or to take some control of the process to assess specific areas which are considered important to family functioning? These preferences will influence which model an individual worker or therapist will select to support their practice. In theory there is a measure of agreement about the aspects of family life which are important and how they interrelate. In practice the methods for working with families differ.

In terms of contemporary practice the government have recently developed a manual to be used for assessing families. This is based on the **Family Assessment Model** (FAM) and includes descriptions of the conceptual framework and very detailed questions which can be used to access the areas of family life described by the model (Bentovin and Bingley Miller, 2002). Rather than try to reproduce this here we would refer practitioners to the original, and will instead describe the **McMaster Model** which was developed before this model and has the same basic components. We think this will be useful to readers who will find the McMaster Model more concise, and hopefully, will find it a useful basis from which to approach the FAM. For those readers who prefer a less structured approach, or who are simply interested in the range of models available, we would refer them to Gurman and Kniskern, 1991.

Whatever the guidelines from agencies, which in the case of health, youth justice and social work are highly structured at the present time, it is important to begin by developing a conceptual framework within which the worker can place the stories and information from the distressed families they will face. The problem oriented approach described here and developed by the McMaster group offers an excellent and fairly safe starting point for those wishing to learn family therapy skills. It also offers a chance to consider core components of family functioning. Throughout this chapter the worker will be referred to as the therapist. However the concepts are relevant to all those engaged in working with people however they wish to describe themselves.

The McMaster Model of Family Functioning

Background

The **McMaster Model of Family Functioning** is a problem-centred marital and family therapy model, which was developed in North America and is not widely available in the UK. It provides a conceptual framework for assessing family functioning and was developed by the McMaster group originally at McGill and McMaster Universities in Canada and currently at Brown University, Providence, USA. The model was developed in a pragmatic way based on extensive clinical experience of working with families. It does not attempt to assess all areas of family functioning but concentrates on those found to be clinically relevant (Miller et al., 2000).

Also based on the McMaster Model is the **Family Assessment Device** (FAD) a 60-item **questionnaire** (Epstein, Baldwin and Bishop, 1983). The FAD is a self-report instrument which can be completed by all family members aged 12 or over. This offers additional information for understanding a family and can provide a baseline for assessing the effectiveness of interventions if administered before and after therapy. The FAD has been widely used on clinical populations including studies on depression (Keitner, Ryan, Miller and Norman, 1992), a cross-cultural study (Keitner, Ryan, Fodor, Miller, Epstein and Bishop, 1990), psychiatric adult inpatients and outpatients (Fristad, 1989), children admitted to a psychiatric day program (Archambault, Doherty, and Bishop, 1990) and a study of adopted and biological children presenting to mental health facilities (Cohen, Coyne and Duvall, 1993). The FAD has also been used to look at family functioning in non-clinical populations, for example, families where a member has Traumatic Brain Injury (Bishop and Miller, 1988) and to identify families at risk in a community sample (Akister and Stevenson-Hinde, 1991).

There is a 12-item **general functioning scale** which is increasingly widely used and now forms part of the assessment strategy which practitioners in Australia use in their child protection assessment (Barber and Deffabbro, 2000).

The model

The McMaster group identify four macro **stages of treatment**:

1. assessment
2. contracting
3. treatment
4. closure

Within these stages there are sub stages, the first of which is always **orientation**. Each therapist will select ways to negotiate these stages and these will to a large degree reflect the therapists' personal style.

The therapy is focussed on the specific problems of the family and it stresses active collaboration of the family members at each stage. Thus the therapists' ideal role is that of catalyst, clarifier and facilitator. The family should be helped to develop awareness of their strengths and to develop problem solving strategies which can be generalised to other situations in the future.

Six to twelve sessions are suggested in order to establish an active involvement by both therapist and family in the process of change. Limiting the number of sessions also communicates to the family confidence in the possibility of change.

We will describe these four stages which form the process of the work undertaken with a family. We will then describe the six **dimensions** of the model in detail. These are the areas of family life which are assessed in detail and are key to informing the process of work with the family, that is the contracting and treatment stages. Finally we will pose questions a therapist might ask in order to assess these dimensions. Thus by the end of this chapter the reader will have a clear idea of the content of this model and some practical knowledge about how to use it.

Assessment

Assessment is the first major stage and consists of four steps:

1. orientation
2. data gathering
3. problem description
4. clarifying and agreeing a problem list

In the assessment the **orientation** is towards beginning the treatment process and to ensuring that the family understand and are willing to be involved in the process which they are undertaking. It is useful to start by getting each family member to give their ideas of why they think they are there and what they are expecting to happen. The therapist can then describe their own ideas, including why they think the family are there, what they plan to do and what they hope to achieve. Sometimes families are referred by other professionals and are not clear why they are there. Once there is clarification the process can begin.

As they move on to **data gathering** the therapist explains that they will be trying to understand how the family functions not only in relation to the presenting problem but in other areas of family life as well. Here the therapist needs the families' permission to ask questions over a range of areas of family life. If the family are uncertain about this it offers a good opportunity to model negotiating skills as the assessment cannot proceed without the families' co-operation. Clarification of the process is time well spent as embarking on assessment without everyone's agreement can alienate one or more family members. Information is then collected to assess the six dimensions of the McMaster Model:

- problem solving
- communication
- roles
- affective responsiveness
- affective involvement
- behaviour control

When the therapist has explored each of these areas (which are described in detail below) the **description of the presenting problem** is revisited and agreed with the family along with any other problems which have been identified in the process of data gathering. Finally a **problem list is agreed** and a decision is made about which problem the family want to tackle first. The emphasis is on co-operation and working together. Thus although the model is highly structured no steps are taken without the family being aware and in agreement with them.

This transparency and shared goal setting is empowering to the families. If the family do not agree with the process the therapy will stop unless a negotiation can be reached.

Contracting

Once there is agreement as to the problems to be tackled a contract needs to be drawn up that describes the process which the family are agreeing to undertake. The steps in the contracting stage are:

- orientation
- outlining options
- negotiating expectations
- contract signing

The therapist **orientates** the family to the new stage and then **outlines the treatment options** at this juncture. It is necessary to present more than one option in order to allow the family to choose their own direction. Clearly treatment options will vary from family to family but the task here is to explore the options (some of which may not need any input from the therapist) and possible consequences. As an example, with the 'B' family one option might be to engage in six sessions to work on those problems which have been agreed in the assessment. Another option could be for the family, having gone through the assessment process and explored what the problems are, to now try and resolve these on their own. The 'B' family then has the task of deciding which option to choose.

We can see practitioners here thinking that the 'B' family, as described, seem very simple and that with more complex families it may be impossible to reach agreement. This may be true and there are two very important points here. Firstly, without agreement to work together progress is unlikely and is unattributable to any effort on the part of the family. Thus, no strategies for the future are learned. Secondly, a family's failure to engage enables both the worker and the family to be clear about the extent of the difficulties and the extent to which the family do not wish to work with the agency on the problems.

At times this may not matter and is merely personal choice. At other times, for example where there are concerns about child protection or abuse of the elderly, failure to engage in the process is diagnostic of the extent of the problems and will aid the workers in the difficult decisions they may have to take.

If the family choose treatment we move on to **negotiating expectations**. This step is where the family negotiate what it is that they want from each other and therefore how they will know that change has been achieved. There is clearly work here for the therapist to ensure that realistic goals are set. For example, goals such as 'Never to fight again' or 'To all be happy' are not attainable and need to be clarified in concrete behavioural terms so that movement towards them can be recognised and valued. This negotiation is crucial to the possibility of successful therapy.

The final step of this stage is to **draw up a written contract**, which lists the problems and those things that have been agreed as satisfactory outcomes.

Treatment

Treatment consists of four steps:

1. orientation
2. clarifying priorities
3. setting tasks
4. task evaluation

As usual the therapist **orientates** the family to the new stage and asks them to **prioritise the problem list**, deciding which problems they want to tackle first. While the therapist may have to intervene if the family ignore urgent problems, it is preferable for the family to decide where they want to start. Taking responsibility for the process is important and emphasises their role as collaborative partners.

The next step is to negotiate and **set a homework task** with the family. The task is to be carried out between sessions and aims to move the family in the direction of their desired goals. The McMaster group outline general principles for negotiating and assigning tasks:

- The task should have maximum potential for success.
- The task should be reasonable with regard to age, sex and sociocultural variables.
- Tasks should be oriented primarily toward increasing positive behaviours rather than increasing negative ones. Families often ask someone to stop their behaviour rather than asking them to do something. We prefer to request positive actions.
- A task should be behavioural and concrete enough so that it can be clearly understood and easily evaluated.
- A task should be meaningful and important to everyone involved.
- Family members should feel that they can accomplish the task and they should individually commit themselves to carry out their part.
- Emotionally oriented tasks should emphasise positive not negative feelings. Fighting, arguing and open display of hostility should be strongly discouraged.
- Tasks should fit reasonably into the families schedule and activities.
- Overloading should be avoided. A maximum of two tasks per session is usually reasonable.
- Assignments to family members should be balanced so that the major responsibility for completing a task does not reside with just one or two members.
- Vindictiveness and digging up the past should be avoided, with the focus placed on constructive dealings with current situations.

(Epstein and Bishop, 1981).

Tasks form the basis of the work the family does together between sessions and **evaluation** at a subsequent session explores whether or not the task was accomplished and its success. If any aspects of the task were found to be difficult these are explored and may be adjusted. If there is a major problem the therapist returns to the assessment and clarifies whether there was really agreement as to the nature of the problems and how the family wish to proceed. If the task has gone well further tasks can be set in relation to the same or other identified problems, to move towards the agreed goals.

While tasks are designed for a specific family problem there are general areas for direct tasks which are compliance based and aim at changing family rules and roles. The therapist expects the family to undertake the tasks set and report back. These tasks might include:

- Coaching parents on how to control children.
- Redistributing jobs among family members.
- Establishing disciplinary rules.
- Providing information.
- Promoting open communication.
- Giving personal feedback.

With the 'B' family we may be looking at coaching parents on how to control children, followed by establishing disciplinary rules. Alternatively, depending on what the assessment reveals, we could be redistributing jobs among family members (altering Grandma's role) and then establishing disciplinary rules. Some family therapists are looking at ways of using email contact between sessions to assist with the treatment stage of therapy (Czaja and Rubert, 2002).

Closure

When the contracted goals are reached or the negotiated number of sessions has occurred, the therapy may move to closure. The steps involved here are:

1. orientation
2. summary of treatment
3. long-term goals
4. follow-up (optional)

There are two objectives to this stage. Firstly, to avoid continuing the therapy without renegotiating the contract. Thus, as the agreed goals are approached, the family reviews its progress and considers whether to stop therapy or whether to define further areas they wish to work on. Secondly, when therapy is ending it is important to **summarise the process** which has been undertaken, and to enable the family to identify the strategies they have learned. In discussing their **long-term goals** they can consider how they will deal with problems in the future, and

think about whether the skills they have used in the present can be applied generally to other situations. It is useful for the therapist to predict that there will be further problems to negotiate in the future, as there are in all families.

Follow-up is optional and may be arranged, although this should be distant enough to transmit confidence in the progress made and should be scheduled as a monitoring, not treatment, session. The steps and stages to be gone through in working with a family are made very clear in this model which describes collaborative working with the family. This is thought to help the partnership between the worker and the family, who gain control over the changes which they need to make to deal with the issues that have arisen. The model, as is common with most family therapy models, does not try to apportion blame for the current difficulties and tries to engage all family members in the process of change.

Dimensions of the McMaster Model

Having described the steps and macro stages involved in working with the family it is time to look at the data gathering needed to assess family functioning. This process, of understanding family functioning, is both an **assessment** and an **intervention**. The therapist is modelling the opportunity for all family members to express their opinions and also making it clear that they are taking time to understand how the family functions, successfully as well as not, before negotiating the desired changes with the family. As described in the section on assessment above, six **dimensions** of family functioning have been identified which should be assessed before any intervention takes place. These dimensions are crucial to the conceptual framework within which the family is approached. A description of each dimension is given followed by a section indicating the kind of questions, which can be used to explore these. All the dimensions should be assessed for strengths, which can be mobilised in therapy as well as for problematic areas.

Problem solving

Problem solving can be defined as the ability of the family to solve problems at a level which maintains effective family functioning. A family problem is one which threatens the way that the family operate (some families have continuing problems which do not threaten their functioning).

Problems can be divided into **instrumental** and **affective**. Instrumental problems are those that concern the more practical and organisational aspects of family life whereas affective problems are more concerned with emotional difficulties. Families who are doing well with the instrumental tasks may have difficulty dealing with emotional areas. It is unusual to find the opposite of this. If there are difficulties with the practicalities of daily living then there are usually also difficulties in handling emotional problems and these families tend to have an overall poorer level of functioning.

Families may be having trouble in a number of dimensions without labelling themselves as dysfunctional. For example they may have difficulty in their roles or in communication function which they have worked around for, maybe, a number of years. However, it seems that if a family are having difficulty with their problem solving this may be the point at which they decide they are not functioning adequately (Akister and Stevenson-Hinde, 1991). It is important to bear this in mind as there is always the temptation for the therapist to feel certain patterns need attention but the family may not agree, as they do not see them as the precipitating factors in the referral.

In exploring problem solving the therapist is interested in the steps which the family go through. These include:

- Problem identification.
- Communication of the problem to the appropriate resource.
- Developing alternative solutions.
- Deciding on a solution.
- Acting on this.
- Monitoring success.

Families do not proceed neatly through these stages or even through all of them when dealing with problems, but they are useful for the therapist to bear in mind as potential steps. The families' problem solving skills should be assessed by looking at problems which the family has solved successfully as well as looking at the presenting problem.

Roles

Roles are defined as the recurrent patterns of behaviour by which individuals fulfil the necessary tasks to maintain family life and enable the development of both the family and the individual within the family. Roles include areas such as:

- Provision of resources.
- Personal development.
- Nurturance and support.
- Adult sexual gratification.
- Maintenance of the family system.

Is the family able to provide food, shelter and maintain financial viability? How do they make financial decisions? Are they able to support personal development by facilitating the children's development from home to school and beyond? It is also important that the adults are allowed to develop or this may pose risks for their wellbeing over time. The family also needs to be able to provide a supportive base for its members although of course they may gain support from outside the family, for example from the extended family, or from friends. Finally there are boundary issues for all families as to who is in the family and how to regulate input, for example, from the grandparent generation (as in the 'B' family above).

All families will have differing ways of approaching these issues and it is important for the therapist to understand each family's role function in order to be able to design appropriate interventions with them. It is also important to consider how appropriate are the allocation of roles and how comfortable family members feel about the allocation. An example of a role allocation which may be dysfunctional is where a child is providing emotional support for an adult, that is, acting as a 'parental child'.

In summary the therapist is concerned to understand the allocation of roles, their appropriateness and how comfortable family members are with this. It is important to respect the culture of the family. Each family finds ways of fulfilling its role function and the therapist's own prefer-ences, for example their views on the male and female division of tasks, need to be set aside.

Communication

Communication is defined as the exchange of information between family members.

Communication is considered on two spec-trums: direct versus indirect and clear versus masked. Thus communication can be:

- clear and direct
- clear and indirect
- masked and direct
- masked and indirect

Clear communication is where the topic of conversation is the topic of concern. So if the speaker is trying to communicate about whose turn it is to clean the bath they raise the subject of whose turn it is to clean the bath. If they are **masked in their communication** they will possibly raise the subject of cleaning without mentioning the bath or may not even raise cleaning and say something like, 'I'm so tired I can't do a thing.' The recipient of this message is left to decipher that it is their turn to clean the bath. It is easy to see that the more masked a message is, the more likelihood of the recipient misinterpreting it, leading to increased tension.

Direct communication is where the com-munication is directed to the appropriate person. So in the example above a **clear direct message** will be: 'John, it's your turn to clean the bath.' A **clear indirect message** will be: 'It must be somebody else's turn to clean the bath.' A **masked indirect message** will be: 'No-one round here ever does any cleaning.'

From this example we can see that the more masked and indirect the communication is, the greater the risk of the message not being received, and if it is received this will not necessarily be by the correct person. It is crucially important to both *ask* people about their communication and also to *observe* what patterns occur during the interview. Both verbal and nonverbal communi-cation should be observed and noted as well as direct or indirect and clear or masked patterns.

Affective responsiveness

Affective responsiveness is an individual di-mension. It is the ability of each family member to respond with affect appropriate to the level of stimuli received. Emotions are divided into **welfare** and **emergency** emotions. Welfare feelings are those such as love, happiness and tenderness; emergency feelings include fear, anger, disappointment and sadness. It is thought that it is important to be able to experience both types of emotion in order to provide an environ-ment where children can develop without re-stricted emotion.

Affective responsiveness should not be confus-ed with affective communication since feelings may be experienced without being com-municated. In our observations, asking family members directly about their responses is often of great interest to each other. This is because feelings are not always shared and family members are often surprised by what others have to say. The opportunity to hear each others' views throughout the assessment is one of the ways an assessment also functions as an agent of change in itself.

For the therapist this is a crucial dimension, as it gives insight into the individuals in the family and may be very important information for designing tasks. So that if, for example, a family member is highly controlled in their expression of anger it is very important to take this into account if tasks are being considered which may stress this and precipitate unsought out-bursts. This has similarity with other emergency responses.

Affective involvement

Affective involvement is the extent to which family members show interest in each others' activities. This dimension overlaps with the concepts of **enmeshed** and **disengaged** families, described by Minuchin (1974). The therapist is concerned here to understand whether family members have things that are important to them outside the family and whether other members can show interest and support without taking over each others' interests.

In some families everyone has to be closely involved all the time (enmeshed) whereas in others there is inadequate interest and support demonstrated (disengaged). Also within the family the closeness of relationships between parents, and between parents and children, should be explored. Although there is no ideal for family life it is crucial to understand how the family you are to work with is placed in this area.

Behaviour control

Behaviour control refers to the mechanisms the family has to control and guide children's and adult's behaviour. Within this model there are three different areas of behaviour control which are of interest for effective family functioning:

1. Physically dangerous situations.
2. Situations which involve meeting psycho-biological needs or drives (e.g. eating, sleeping, aggression).
3. Situations involving interpersonal socialising behaviour.

In assessing behaviour control the therapist tries to see what behaviour is deemed acceptable within this family and how these standards are maintained for both adults and children.

Behaviour control can be considered within four styles:

- Rigid Behaviour Control – where standards are very restricted and there is little room for negotiating.
- Flexible Behaviour Control – involves reasonable standards and a degree of flexibility given the context.
- Laissez-Faire Behaviour Control – refers to those families where standards do not really exist and where almost 'anything goes'.
- Chaotic Behaviour Control – is found in families where there is no consistent style. In these families members cannot be sure what response to expect.

Flexible behaviour control is thought to be the most effective style, with rigid next, then laissez-faire, and lastly chaotic behaviour control.

Questions a therapist might ask

All therapists develop their own style and ways of establishing rapport and collecting information from families. When starting out, the process can be daunting, and the therapist overwhelmed, by the amount of material produced in a family interview. To assess a family on the lines described above and to ensure a facilitative, enabling approach at all stages will take two or three separate sessions. It is imperative to plan these sessions and we think it is helpful to consider the kind of questions you may ask. Even experienced therapists fall into the trap of exploring some areas and excluding others, and it is helpful to refresh your understanding of any model by referring back to the basic concepts. To help with this, questions are included which could be asked for each dimension and which can be revisited when one is stuck in work with a particular family. There are no 'right' or 'wrong' answers and the skill is in finding ways to understand family life, through the interview process, and in a way, which is transparent to the family. (The transparency and partnership is also a feature of the FAM (Bentovim and Bingley Miller, 2002), but is not a feature of all models.)

The questions which follow are taken from the **McMaster Structured Interview Schedule** (Bishop et al., 1987). This interview was designed for research and teaching purposes. It is an extremely useful learning exercise to work through all these questions with a family (both for the family and therapist) and we would highly recommend this. In addition all therapists have areas they find difficult to explore with families and using a structured interview offers a way of exploring this to the benefit of the family you are working with. However, we do recognise that people will not always want to undertake the whole interview and it can be helpful to use selected dimensions once you have a grasp of the presenting difficulties.

As the focus of the model is to understand the families' strengths, as well as the current problem, there is an emphasis on understanding their normal procedures. Thus, for example, in problem solving the concern is not just the presenting problem but what the normal, successful problem solving processes of the family are in order to understand what is different and that has led to the presenting problem.

The therapists' style is important since it models **clarifying** and **facilitating**. The therapist should always feedback what they think the family have told them to check that the information they are receiving is actually what the family is trying to communicate. It is surprising how often the family will correct the therapist's perceptions demonstrating how difficult it is to accurately communicate family relationships.

The McMaster Structured Interview Schedule (McSIS)

The entire **McSIS** can be found in the article by Bishop et al. (1987). The questions included here give a flavour of the kinds of questions used by McSIFF and by FAM (Bentovim and Bingley Miller, 1987) when assessing the dimensions of family functioning. They are included in order to give a clear idea of the kinds of questions which we need to explore with families when undertaking a family assessment and to lend a practical approach to these difficult areas of family life.

Orientation

Begin by explaining that as well as exploring the presenting problem you would like to ask questions over a range of subjects in order to understand how the family functions in all areas. Ask permission to do this. If permission is not forthcoming the therapist needs to explore this with the family, giving a clear explanation of why they want to understand the families functioning over a range of areas and not just in relation to the presenting problem. The orientation may take a few minutes or may need a lot of time. This time is well used since it sets the style of the therapy as a partnership, negotiated with the family, rather than something imposed on them.

Problem solving

Explore the presenting problem and if possible other problems. Ask questions, such as:

- When did you first notice the problem?
- Who first noticed the problem?
- Is this the person who usually notices problems?
- Is this the way problems usually get noticed in your family?
- When you noticed the problem did you tell anyone?
- Who did you tell?
- How have you tried to solve the problem?
- Did you think of other ways to deal with the problem?
- How did you decide what to do?
- Was the decision discussed with the person who was affected by the decision?
- Is this usually the way the family decides what to do?
- Once you decided on your course of action did you actually carry it out?
- Do you usually carry out your decisions?
- Did you check to see that things got done after you decided what to do about the problem?
- Would you say this is typical of how you deal with most family problems?
- How well do you think you did with this problem?
- Did you learn anything from solving this problem that might help you with others in the future?
- Just to review then: do you feel most problems get dealt with quickly and efficiently in your family?

Roles

Next ask some questions about how jobs around the house get shared out. Ask the family if this is ok? This orients the family to a change of subject and checks that they are in agreement. Questions could cover:

Provision of resources

In terms of the day-to-day organisation who is involved in the various family jobs and whether they get done or not? Some topics which could be explored are listed below:

- shopping
- cooking
- cleaning
- garden
- paying bills and handling money
- dealing with cars
- large purchases
- repairs round house
- deals with school

Role allocation

- Does the family discuss who is to do the various jobs?
- Does anyone feel they have too many jobs?
- Is anyone doing a job they shouldn't be?
- Does anyone refuse to do assigned duties?

Role accountability

Does the family feel that jobs in the house are generally well handled by their family?

Personal development

Are both parents equally involved in bringing up the children? If young children which of them is typically involved in:

- Getting children up and dressed?
- Baths, shampooing hair?
- Putting children to bed?
- Taking them out?
- Talking to the children?

If school age children which of them is typically involved in:

- Talking to the children?
- Parent/teacher/school meetings?
- Discussion of career choice?

To the parent who is least involved:

Do they also get involved in dealing with bringing up the children?

Management of the system:

If a decision has to be made and you disagree who would usually have the last word?

To both partners:

- How much do they see their parents or extended family?
- Do they see them too much or too little? Any problems?
- Do they have problems with each other's families?

Nurturance and support:

To each individual:

- When things get to them or they've had a bad day who do they go to?

For small children:
Who do the kids usually go to when upset?

Adult gratification:

Do they feel comfortable with the amount of affection they get from each other?

(If there is a sexual problem this will need to be discussed without the children present).

Behaviour control

Ask questions about the rules and standards they have as a family, say: is that okay?

Starting with the children:

- Do they know what time mum and dad expect them to be in bed? (Is that the same for everyone?)
- Do they know what things mum and dad would think were dangerous?
- What are those things. Examples might be crossing the road, playing with matches.
- Are people in their family allowed to hit each other?
- Do they know what to expect when children break a rule?
- Do the parents agree on the rules?

To the Parents:

- Do they feel the therapist has got the right picture?
- Do they generally agree about the rules?

- Do they generally react in the same way? Are they consistent?
- Do they feel supported by their partner when disciplining the children?

Behaviour Control for adults:

- Are the rules for adults clear?
- Does anyone overdo things?

Communication

Explore both instrumental and affective communication.

- clear/masked
- direct/indirect

How much time is the family awake and together as a family?

Do they have enough time for talking as a family?

Parents:

- How much time do the two parents spend talking with each other?
- Are they satisfied with the amount of time?
- Do any of them feel they have difficulty in the way they talk to each other?
- Does the family talk about moods and feelings much?
- Can individuals talk about feelings?

(Observe verbal and non-verbal communication throughout all interviews).

Affective responsiveness

For each family member: ask for examples and rephrase for children:

- Can they tell you about a time or experience that gave them a sense of pleasure?
- Can they tell you about a time when they felt tenderness or concern for someone else?
- Do they ever get angry?
- Are there situations where they feel sad?
- What are their responses for the various situations or do they over or under react?

Affective involvement

To each family member:

- What things are important to them?
- Are others in the family interested in what they do?
- Does anyone feel that another family member is too close to, or interested in them?
- How often does each go out on their own, or out together without the children

To adults:

- Do you feel the relationship with your child/children is close enough?
- Do you ever feel it is too close?
- Do you feel your relationship with your spouse is close enough?

Closure

- Does the family think the therapist has a reasonable idea of how the family functions?
- Is there anything else they feel the therapist should know about the family that hasn't been covered?

These questions give the therapist an opportunity to gather information with the family about the six dimensions. It is then possible to return to the problem description stage of assessment described above. All this information, plus any that was gathered earlier when exploring the presenting problem, can be used to agree what is to happen next and to work out with them ways to try and get there.

We have taken a long look at the components of assessing a family. The McMaster model that has been described allows an opportunity to develop partnership with the family and an empowering approach. Clearly there will be times when practitioners have to make difficult decisions but the transparency of this assessment approach and also of the more complex approach of the FAM (Bentovin and Bingley Miller, 2002) mean that the family are engaged in these difficult realisations as far as possible.

Time taken to assess, or understand, is never wasted: it allows the family to realise that their difficulties are being taken seriously and that someone wants to hear their story. At times families or parents feel they cannot make their voice heard and the assessment process is a key opportunity for this. It is also helpful to ensure that the same interventions are not tried again with families who have been seen by a number of other professionals already.

In the models where work with the family begins after a less comprehensive assessment, part of the process of therapy usually involves gathering information from the experience of homework tasks. If a task fails what exactly went wrong and why? The answer is often based in the setting of tasks which challenged the structure of the family too much due to not fully understanding their patterns of functioning. This is a less systematic approach and does not involve the same kind of open partnership as proposed by the McMaster model and FAM. Overall we feel that the more a family feel heard and engaged with the workers, and the more information that the workers have about the family functioning, the more likelihood of a successful and speedy outcome to the therapy.

This chapter has proposed a model for this work and suggested questions that may be asked to facilitate the process. There are many other ways to approach families and we hope that ideas from this assessment protocol will help all practitioners working with families.

CHAPTER 5

Socially Inclusive Practice

Introduction

One of the modern critiques of family therapy practice is that, along with many psycho-therapeutic orientations in contemporary practice, it fails to address the broader structural issues that affect the way people live and the problems experienced by families. The discussion in some journals and books becomes limited to simplistic characterisations of therapeutic approaches as out of touch, or radical practice that is naive. This is not helpful if you recognise that each approach has some merit and you have the intellectual flexibility to use approaches that fit with the circumstances presented. The task is to find the right combination of methods, and models of work, that can make a difference to a particular family with a particular problem, at a particular time. This is preferable to wasting effort in justifying a universal approach or trying to suggest that all problems are due to social inequalities.

Another objection raised to family therapy or any other psycho-therapeutic orientation is that it is unrealistic or even dangerous to attempt such approaches. This is because either they: a) are not within the remit of the service specification of the agency, or, b) that practitioners should not dabble in areas that require advanced training to be employed competently. As far as the first point is concerned there is ample evidence that modern family support practised in all its agency manifestations is expected to go beyond narrow resource-driven service. Practitioners understand the need to bring to bear a range of knowledge, skills and values to the problems faced by citizens who, through no fault of their own, find themselves in need of help and support. Whether it is government guidance, legislation, or professional ethical codes of practice, there are plenty of examples exhorting staff to work and think therapeutically.

The second point is disingenuous because many people enter professional training with experience and skills that ideally suit a family therapy approach. And you do not have to have completed advanced clinical training to be able to use some relatively simple concepts and techniques in your work with families that can reflect systems theory within the limits of safe, accountable practice. For example, access to a suitably qualified specialist for consultation or supervision ensures the work can be monitored and your practice evaluated. It is possible to employ some of the key concepts and theoretical ideas from family therapy in relatively straightforward pieces of work that can make a big difference. The key idea is that you are *thinking* systemically and therefore using a different paradigm in which to practice: not that you are claiming expertise that you do not have or you are experimenting on powerless service users.

As we have already noted earlier in this book, the basic psycho-social framework of modern caring practice is complementary to the systems theory that underpins family therapy practice. No practitioner can be effective without combining the individual psychology of the client with the social context of their problems. Similarly, no family therapist can properly work with a family's internal problems in the absence of the wider context of their experience. Nor is this necessarily an advocacy for burdening practitioners with the task of remedying the inadequacies of capitalist economics, it is rather a means of engaging with service users at the level of their daily life. Grounding your work in the family's ordinariness can equally dismiss the criticisms of therapeutic approaches as being divorced from reality in abstract conceptual thinking. The skill is employing what can be obtuse ideas in a meaningful and relevant way. This is why it is crucial to consider socially inclusive ways of working with families.

The term **social inclusion** has gained rapid acceptance within the caring profession lexicon at the beginning of the twenty-first century. It began to appear prominently in political discourse in the UK following the election of a Labour government in 1997 which regarded social exclusion as an impediment to its vision of a more open and equal society concerned with social justice as well as economic progress (Walker, 2003). The concept of social exclusion has its origins in France in the 1970s where the idea of citizenship and social cohesion highlighted the plight of Les exclus who were relegated to the margins of society (Barry and Hallett, 1998; Pierson, 2002). The social policy aim therefore is to advance a socially inclusive social and health care policy enabling every family to enjoy the opportunities offered by late capitalist Britain and the European Economic Community in an increasingly economically globalised world. This should fit with an empowering practice.

Each family, regardless of class, race, culture, age, religion, disability or gender should find the traditional barriers to their advancement being dismantled so that nobody is excluded from sharing in the wealth and resources being offered at a time of sustained economic expansion. These political aspirations fit with the value base of caring work which embodies anti-discriminatory practice, respect for persons, and equal opportunities for every citizen. However just as the earlier stages of capitalism resulted in new approaches to the social management of the disruption, impoverishment, and alienation of the social casualties of economic progress, so too are the late stages of capitalism (Leonard, 1997).

The evidence confirms that the gap between rich and poor is widening, there are more children living in poverty, the prison population is at its highest recorded level, and disabled people are more likely to live in poverty or be unemployed than non-disabled people. Children from working class families are less likely to receive a further or higher education and black families are more likely to live in poor housing. There are however differences within these broad examples of social exclusion that need to be taken into account when you are assessing strengths, resources, and gaps in social networks where you are trying to help. For example, inner city deprivation, migration patterns, and poorer health outcomes are factors also associated with class and are therefore likely to affect any family in disadvantaged social circumstances.

Practitioners are among those in the front line, faced with the consequences of the failure of this latest social policy aspiration and the raised expectations of families in need. Evidence suggests that the process of exclusion continued in the 1970s as rising levels of poverty began to be quantified. In the process a new role has evolved for family support work not so much as a provider of services or even as a therapeutic intervention but rather as a front-line service focussed on the management of exclusion and rationing of scarce resources (Jones, 1997). This has always been an uncomfortable position for practitioners who subscribe to an empowering model of practice that seeks to challenge social injustice. However, there are numerous positions in non-statutory, independent, voluntary or charitable organisations, where fewer constraints permit practice that is not defined in reductionist ways. And even within statutory contexts, there are more opportunities for using systems theory than might at first appear to be the case.

Family therapy and social development

The idea of family therapy practice and social development is based on the premise that most people's problems are sorted out within and between their existing local network of friends, relatives and neighbours. Thus the link with systems theory and family therapy can be drawn: the focus of attention is wider than the individual presenting difficulty or the intra-familial dynamics. You have a role in seeking to reinforce and support those networks or helping to facilitate their growth where they have declined, as a protective and preventive strategy. Community practice informed by systems theory is therefore an excellent intervention strategy for promoting social inclusion. Thus, widening the focus of orthodox family therapy means working with every possible part of the wider system that is part of the community experiencing social exclusion. It does not as is sometimes assumed, exclude work with individuals. The spectrum of activity includes (Smale et al., 2000):

- **Direct intervention** – work carried out with individuals, families and local networks to tackle problems that directly affect them.
- **Indirect intervention** – work with community groups and other professionals and agencies to tackle problems affecting a range of people.
- **Change agent activity** – this seeks to change the ways that people relate to each other and that are responsible for social problems, whether at individual, family or neighbourhood levels, by reallocating resources.
- **Service delivery activity** – providing services that help to maintain people in their own homes, to reduce risks to vulnerable people, and provide relief to parents or carers.

Systems theory that informs community practice is not just about transforming neighbourhoods whether on small or large scales, but it can also enable personal change and growth in individuals through social action and the fostering of co-operative activity. The reverse of course is also true. Individual work using family therapy concepts that focus on the internal problems of children and families can also contribute to wider social transformation in neighbourhoods. Once change occurs in separate families it can cascade throughout a street, tower block or estate. Defining community work in its widest sense and holding a systems perspective includes anything from visiting lonely housebound people, setting up a food co-operative, and establishing a collective resource such as a credit union. It could also involve helping to organise a protest march to the Town Hall to lobby for improvements to neighbourhood services and community safety (Thompson, 2002; Adams et al., 2002).

With such broad definitional parameters it is not surprising to conclude that there is a shortage of reliable empirical data about activity in this area of practice (Macdonald, 1999). Without a common understanding of community practice it is hard to quantify and compare the outcomes for evaluative purposes. The available evidence does suggest, however, that it is community-oriented, pro-active initiatives that are most valued by citizens and are doing most in helping to support families and individuals in need. A modern family therapy model offers the appropriate holistic perspective for practitioners to engage with other professionals in the community, to work in partnership with families, and employ the personal relationship skills the majority of practitioners aspire to use.

It cannot be overstated that your practice in family therapy should always take account of the impact the wider social policy context is having on you and the family you are attempting to help. As well as the internal dynamics of the individuals and their patterns of relationships, your assessment should include the effects of e.g. long-term unemployment or drug abuse, or poor housing conditions on the capacity to parent and relate. Equally it is helpful if you consider what impact various statutory regulations and procedural guidance is having on shaping your work and your beliefs about service users. This is not to add more confusion to possibly complex and difficult casework, but to enable a more sensitive and tailor-made intervention to be designed so that it harmonises with the family's real day-to-day experience. Clients will recognise this and feel properly listened to, valued, understood and be more ready to engage in work than if you try to apply a rigid, inflexible, model of practice.

Black and ethnic minority families

Inspection of services for black children and their families in Britain shows that despite years of

rhetoric of anti-racist and anti-oppressive practice, assessments and care planning are still
generally inadequate. The guidance suggests:

▨ *Ensuring that services and staffing are monitored
by ethnicity to ensure they are provided appropriately and equally.*
▨ *Involving ethnic minorities in planning and reviewing services.*
▨ *Training in anti-racist and anti-discriminatory
practice.*
▨ *Investigating and monitoring complaints of racial
discrimination or harassment.*
▨ *Ensuring explicit policies are in place for working
with black families.*

(SSI, 2000)

Practitioner's skills in facilitating service user
empowerment are indicated in any vision of the
future shape of service provision (Walker, 2001c).
A family therapy practice framework employing
community work can enable black families and
young people to support each other and raise
collective awareness of shared issues. Investigation
of indigenous healing practices and beliefs provide
a rich source of information to utilise in the
helping process. Advocacy skills in which young
people are encouraged to be supported and
represented by advocates of their choice with a
children's rights perspective, would help contribute to influencing current service provision
(Ramon, 1999). Systems theory and family
therapy practice that links the internal and
external world of the client, augmented with
culturally competent skills, can better meet the
needs of socially excluded children and families.

Continual reflection and evaluation of practice
is required to maintain an anti-racist socially-
inclusive practice. Recognising racial harassment
as a child protection issue and as an indicator for
subsequent potential mental health problems is
evidence for example, of how you can translate
policy generalisation into specific practice change.
Practitioners who make sure they take full
account of a child's religion, racial, cultural and
linguistic background in the decision making
process are demonstrating the link between social
policy and socially inclusive practice. Ensuring
for example, that black children in residential care

have positive role models and access to advocates
can assist in challenging institutionally racist
practice.

Anti-racist and anti-oppressive practice will
help develop strategies to overcome value judgments about the superiority of white British
family culture and norms. Exploring the impact
of white power and privileges in professional
relationships with black people, and drawing
connections between racism and the social control elements of practice, is another example.
Rejecting stereotypes of black and ethnic minority family structures and relationships will enable
you to assess the rich cultural, linguistic and
spiritual diversity of family life and permit the
building of family therapy assessment and intervention practice that is not based on a deficit
model judged against an anglocentric norm. Not
only will your practice be enriched but black
families will more easily engage with your helping
efforts.

Young offenders

Young offenders are among the most socially
excluded groups in society and the evidence
suggests that imprisonment simply makes matters
worse not better. Within two years of release, 75
per cent will have been reconvicted and 47 per
cent will be back in jail (Social Exclusion Unit,
2002). If some of these young people become
homeless or end up in insecure accommodation,
they are between eight and 11 times more likely to
develop mental health problems (Stephens, 2002).
Young offenders are three times as likely to have a
mental health problem as other young people. Yet
these problems are often neglected because there
are no proper methods for screening and assessing
mental health problems within the youth justice
system (Farrington, 1995; Goodman and Scott,
1997; Royal College of Psychiatrists, 2002;
Mental Health Foundation, 2002). Your assessment and intervention practice, based on systems
thinking, can make a huge difference to this
vulnerable group of young people by:

▨ Encouraging multi-agency decision-making
meetings to consider the wider context of the
young person.

- Articulating the psychological and mental health needs of young offenders as part of dysfunctional family dynamics.
- Offering supportive interventions and diversionary activities to young people at risk.
- Combining and networking with like-minded staff from other agencies to offer groupwork or family therapy to disaffected youth.

The evidence shows that more than 25 per cent of young men and 41 per cent of young women under 21 in prison had received treatment for mental health problems in the year before they were jailed (Lader et al., 1997). Once in the prison system, a lack of purposeful activity, long hours in cells, and a climate of brutality and bullying can reinforce negative attitudes and magnify underlying mental health problems. Prison is no place for young people where isolation militates against family or group communication skills that are essential for the rehabilitation process. The risk of suicide is all too evident, with frequent reports of suicide in young offenders' institutions. Even the most progressive regimes are inadequate to the task of meeting these already damaged individuals' needs for stability, certainty, care, and proper support to tackle their offending behaviour within a context of restorative justice and personal responsibility, backed up by therapeutic input.

Looked after children

Nearly 60,000 children were being looked after by local authorities for the year ending 2001. About 60 per cent of these children had been abused or neglected, with a further ten per cent coming from 'dysfunctional families' (DoH 2001). Abuse of this nature can lead to self-harming behaviour, severe behavioural problems and depression all of which militate against engaging in family processes. Of these 60,000, 38,400 children were in foster placements and 6,400 were in children's homes, yet foster carers and residential staff are among the least qualified and supported people and left to manage sometimes extreme behaviour. Their explanatory models and attempts at managing difficult behav-

iour could reinforce negative patterns of interaction and undermine a more useful family therapy approach. Family therapy approaches are probably nowhere more indicated and yet nowhere least likely to be offered. A practitioner employing systems theory could offer just enough support to carers to help them understand and find ways of coping.

A recent research study emphasised the importance of a preventive approach with children in the public care system that are more likely to be excluded from school following emotional and behavioural difficulties (Fletcher-Campbell, 2001). Teacher training that fails to adequately prepare newly-qualified staff to respond to the mental health needs of pupils is considered to be a factor in the increased use of school exclusions (OFSTED, 1996). Practitioners using a family therapy approach could be helpful to teaching staff and organise collaborative work aimed at preventing difficult behaviour escalating. Unless the mental health needs of these children and young people are addressed as part of a strategy that effectively nurtures children's inclusion in school the risk of deterioration is high. The risk factors for looked after children are probably the most extreme of any socially excluded group: therefore it is crucial to put effort in to prevent problem behaviour escalating (Richardson and Joughin, 2000).

Refugees and asylum seekers

Refugees and asylum seeking people are among the most disadvantaged ethnic minority group for whom culturally competent practice is essential. Some are unaccompanied, and many are affected by extreme circumstances such as witnessing the murder of parents or kin, dislocation from school and community, and severing of important friendships. Lack of extended family support, loss of home, and prolonged insecurity add to their sense of vulnerability. These experiences can trigger symptoms of post traumatic stress syndrome and a variety of mental health problems (Dwivedi, 2002).

Parents' coping strategies and overall resilience can be diminished in these trying circumstances, disrupting the self-regulatory patterns of comfort and family support usually available at times of stress. Your involvement needs to take a broad holistic and systems approach to intervention and not overlook the need for careful assessment of mental health problems developing in adults and children, whilst responding to practical demands. If these are not tackled promptly these people may go on to develop serious and persistent difficulties which are harder, and more costly to resolve, in the long term.

The number of applications for asylum from unaccompanied under-18s almost trebled between 1997 and 2001 from 1,105 to 3,469. DoH figures indicate that there were 6,750 unaccompanied asylum-seeking children supported by local authorities in 2001. Further evidence shows that many of these young people were accommodated and receiving a worse service than other children in need (Audit Commission, 2000). Very little research has been done to ascertain the needs of this group of children. However there is some evidence of the symptoms of post traumatic stress syndrome being present before they then experience the racist and xenophobic abuse of individuals and institutions incapable of demonstrating humanitarian concern for their plight. This combination can shatter the most psychologically robust personality. It has been estimated that serious mental health disorders may be present in 40–50 per cent of young refugees (Hodes, 1998).

Romanies, Gypsies and Travellers may be included in recent groups of asylum and refugee-seeking families escaping ethnic 'cleansing' in the Balkan region of Central and Eastern Europe (Walker, 2003). These families have a long history of persecution and flight from discrimination. Roma, Gypsy and Traveller families who have for many years made their home in Britain are probably one of the most socially excluded groups of people living in Britain. Unemployment among these groups is in the region of 70 per cent, while increasing numbers of their children are failing to complete even a basic education (Save the Children, 2001). These factors – particularly the lack of proper education, are risk factors for the development of psycho-social problems. The overall context of social exclusion means an absence of contact with preventive services or the positive interaction with peers necessary for developmental attainment. Sensitive family therapy work can help families begin the process of re-establishing patterns of behaviour that can sustain and nurture the personal growth of all concerned. Effort is required to enhance the engagement process with these families by:

- Gaining an understanding of the concept of culture.
- Appreciating your own culture.
- Desiring to facilitate effective communication.
- Appreciating the varying perceptions of family process across cultures.
- Desiring to work with families by considering their cultural values.

The family life cycle

We noted in Chapter 2 that orthodox family therapy takes the family life cycle concept as a significant framework for studying the predictable stages through which all families pass. This framework draws upon a variety of theoretical resources to integrate individual developmental tasks, sociological concepts, and clinical research (Carter and McGoldrick, 1999). Using a family life cycle framework means assessing at what stage the family are when they come to your attention or present with particular difficulties to your agency. Families are understood to be evolving through a series of regular transitional stages involving marriage and partnership, birth of children, adolescent independence, leaving home, parental maturity, older age and bereavement. Some family therapists conceptualise problems as occurring at transitional points in the life cycle that the family are finding particularly stressful. This causes the family system to attempt to re-define itself as structural changes begin that upset the existing equilibrium. Thus a family will hesitate at a transitional point and produce an individual member with symptomatic behaviour to prevent the transition. The therapist's task is to assess the developmental stage and intervene to help the family to move on to the next stage.

Another way of looking at the concept of the family life cycle is to regard it as a more positive resource with which to understand the capacity of the family to retain its stability and continuity whilst under stress from negotiating a stage. In this regard the family is viewed as having innate resilience to use its strengths and interpersonal processes to overcome the required transitions. The more resilient the family the more successfully it reorganises to manage disruptions (Glantz and Johnson, 1999). However, both of these conceptualisations pay insufficient attention to the social context of family life cycle transitions. Class and ethnicity are crucial determining factors that influence to a large degree the capacity of families to manage and negotiate already potentially stressful experiences. Class determines how many options, opportunities, and privileges are open to them, as well as the resources for coping with foreseeable or unforeseeable transitions (Rank, 2000).

It is very important also to consider whether this model of the family life cycle is applicable to every family you encounter. The timing of life cycle changes will vary between families from different ethnic backgrounds. The tasks that are considered appropriate will depend on the specific traditions, rituals and ceremonies particular to different cultures. A socially inclusive family therapy practice needs to assess the degree of ethnic identification, social class, religion, politics and geographical background influencing their patterns of behaviour. The length of time spent in this country since immigration and the degree to which they value past traditions are crucially important factors to take into account. The different generations will all hold subtle or major differences in the degree to which they can accommodate and adapt to a new language and cultural context. This in itself can create tensions and disputes that will affect life cycle stages.

It is argued that differences in basic assumptions about western and eastern concepts of self, need to be explicitly acknowledged in order to avoid mistakes in seeking to engage ethnic minority families. Western views emphasise independence, self-sufficiency, assertiveness and competition, with clear, direct verbal communication. Eastern views emphasise interdependence, harmony and co-operation in relationships with more emphasis on non-verbal indirect communication (Lau,

1995). Spiritual and religious beliefs have not featured much in the traditional family therapy or caring literature, yet for many families these are central organising contexts affecting behaviour and relationships. Religious leaders offer an initial focus for many families in trouble; for example, the Rabbi in Orthodox Jewish communities and the Imam in Muslim communities are central figures.

In order to practice in an inclusive way using systems theory requires you to suspend your own assumptions about family process and focus on the particular family without stereotyping or negating their special cultural idiosyncrasies. Grandparents may hold a powerful role in some families while senior male figures and siblings are expected to have authority and responsibility over others. Parental relationships may be ostensibly based on inequality but on closer examination reveal subtle power differences depending on the context. The important point is that your practice is based on the foundational practices of caring work: respect for persons, and positive regard, combined with a systems framework that enables you to seek out and value the unique characteristics of the family you aspire to help.

Cultural competence

There is growing interest in the development of multi-disciplinary and interprofessional working in order to maximise the effectiveness of interventions to meet the diverse needs of multi-cultural societies and service users (Magrab et al., 1997; Oberheumer, 1998; Tucker et al., 1999). The characteristics of such work apply in a framework familiar to practitioners. It begins with assessment then proceeds through decision-making, planning, monitoring, evaluation, and finally to closure. It is argued that this common framework offers the optimum model for encouraging reflective practice to be at the core of contemporary practice (Taylor and White, 2000; Walker, 2002). Reflective practice offers the opportunity to shift beyond functional analysis to making active links between the value base, policy-making process, and the variety of interventions conducted. It also fits in with the open, flexible characteristics of family therapy practice.

Combining reflective practice with culturally competent practice, practitioners have the opportunity to make a major contribution towards responding to the social policy aspiration of inclusion and anti-oppressive practice. In so doing you can facilitate closer co-operation between professionals coming into contact with vulnerable families on a shared agenda of challenging institutional and personal discrimination (Eber et al., 1996; VanDenBerg and Grealish, 1996; Sutton, 2000). One of the defining features of good practice is the ability to work closely with other professionals and communities, often in a co-ordinating role or as a client advocate. Systems theory offers the appropriate conceptual model for evaluating those inter-agency relationships that can foster or hinder collaborative working. This role in the context of work with a variety of problems and contexts is crucial at various points of the intervention process to ensure culturally competent practice.

Drawing together the elements of practice that can contribute towards a model of culturally competent care means it is possible to define cultural competence as a set of knowledge-based and interpersonal skills that allow individuals to understand, appreciate and work with families from cultures other than their own. Five components have been identified (Kim, 1995) comprising culturally competent care:

- Awareness and acceptance of cultural differences.
- Capacity for cultural self-awareness.
- Understanding the dynamics of difference.
- Developing basic knowledge about the family's culture.
- Adapting practice skills to fit the cultural context of the child and family.

These are consistent with other work which critique the historical development of cross-cultural services and offer a model of service organisation and development designed to meet the needs of black and ethnic minority families (Dominelli, 1988; Moffic and Kinzie, 1996; Bhugra, 1999; Bhugra and Bahl, 1999). Culture has been defined as the sets of shared cultural perspectives, meanings, and adaptive behaviours derived from simultaneous membership and participation in a multiplicity of contexts such as geographical, religious, ethnicity, language, race, nationality and ideology. It has also been described as the knowledge, values, perceptions and practices that are shared among the members of a given society, and passed on from one generation to the next (Leighton, 1981). Four particular theories have been identified that are used in modern family therapy practice that attempt to harmonise systems theory with cultural competence (Falicov, 1995):

- **Ethnic focussed** – this stresses that families differ but assumes that the diversity is primarily due to ethnicity. It focuses on the commonality of thoughts, behaviour, feelings, customs and rituals that are perceived as belonging to a particular ethnic group.
- **Universalist** – this asserts that families are more alike than they are different. Hence, universalist norms are thought to apply to all families.
- **Particularist** – this believes that all families are more different than they are alike. No generalisations are possible, each family is unique.
- **Multi-dimensional** – this goes beyond the one-dimensional definition of culture as ethnicity, and aims at a more comprehensive and complex definition of culture that embraces other contextual variables.

An attempt to elaborate a theoretical framework for multi-cultural counselling and therapy suggests that an overarching theory needs to be employed that permits different theoretical models to be applied and integrated. In this way, both practitioner and family identities can be embedded in multiple levels of life experiences with the aim of enabling greater account being taken of the client's experience in relation to their context. The power differentials between worker and service users are recognised as playing an important role in the therapeutic relationship. Clients are helped by developing a greater awareness of themselves in relation to their different contexts resulting in therapy that is contextual in orientation and draws upon traditional healing practices (Sue et al., 1996).

Ethnocentric and particularly Eurocentric, explanations of emotional and psychosocial development are not inclusive enough to understand the development of diverse ethnic minority groups. Failure to understand the cultural background of families can lead to unhelpful assessments, non-compliance, poor use of services, and alienation of the individual or family from the welfare system. Practitioners using an anti-discriminatory, empowerment model of family therapy practice are ideally placed to work with other professionals in multi-disciplinary contexts to enable the team to maintain a focus on culturally competent practice. For example, the increased demand for help from parents and children themselves suffering the effects of mental health problems has prompted policy initiatives to invest in and reconfigure child and adolescent mental health service provision in more acceptable and accessible ways.

The aim is to make them more accessible and acceptable to all cultures by improving multi-agency working (House of Commons, 1997; Davis et al., 1997; Mental Health Foundation, 1999). However, in order to be effective all staff need to address the different belief systems and explanatory thinking behind psychological symptoms. Your family therapy skills and caring values are required to articulate these concepts in such teams. Challenging crude stereotypes, questioning implicit racism and simply ensuring that other staff stop and think about their assumptions can help. Combined with respectful consideration of indigenous healing practices within diverse populations this can optimise helping strategies. The traditional methods and models of family therapy practice failed to take full account of cultural factors but contemporary literature is attempting to catch up. The following areas offer guidance to enhance your communication skills (Whiting, 1999):

- Families may have different styles of communicating fear, grief, anxiety, concern and disagreement.
- Emphasis should be placed on listening, with the goal of understanding the family's perspective.

- Care should be taken to explain to the family the agency culture.
- Steps should be taken to recognise and resolve conflicts which occur between the cultural preferences, understandings and practices recommended by professionals.
- Communication is enhanced if you can demonstrate sensitivity towards the family's cultural values.
- Appreciating the family's cultural understanding of the problem will help build a trusting relationship.

Case illustration

A family of Iraqi asylum seekers fled the country before the recent American and British invasion in 2003. The father Mohammad had worked in a civil service position in a government agency connected to the petroleum industry. He had been accused of passing information to the UN regarding breaches of the sanctions imposed on the use of oil revenues. Mohammad claims he was tortured and had death threats made against his wife and three children. The children are all under ten years of age and his wife Saleha is a nursery teacher. Some of the children speak very little English. The family have been dispersed to a market town in a northern county where there are very few Iraqis, or any families from Middle Eastern countries. The local Housing Department have referred the family to your office following reports of racist attacks on the run-down council estate where they have been housed in emergency accommodation. A teacher has called your team three times in the past fortnight expressing concern about one of the children who is wetting and soiling in class, provoking bullying and humiliating behaviour from other children.

Commentary

Using a systems perspective your first task is to make a map of all the people, agencies and services connected to this family. You will find it helpful to then make contact with as many as you can within a realistic timescale to start to plan your response. Figure 5.1 illustrates this concept. This information-gathering exercise will enable you to begin to evaluate the different agendas and

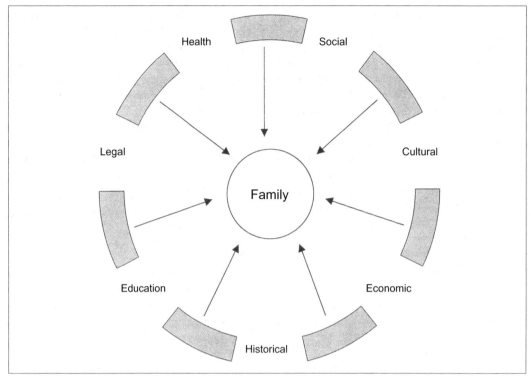

Figure 5.1: Multiple systems impacting on families

perceptions of other staff working with or concerned with the family. Your priority is to establish meaningful contact with the family and gain factual evidence of racist incidents for possible criminal prosecution against the perpetrators, as well as offering a caring, sympathetic relationship. Bear in mind that the family are likely to be highly suspicious of your motives and will require a lot of genuine evidence that they should trust you. Their naturally defensive behaviour may come across as hostile or uncommunicative and you need to deal with this in a non-confrontational manner. A translator or interpreter should accompany you, having been fully briefed beforehand about your task, the different roles each member of your team holds, and to assess their suitability for this particular task. Do not assume that every interpreter is the same: try to evaluate their beliefs or attitudes and whether there may be ethnic or religious differences between them and the family. For a variety of reasons they might be inappropriate for this task despite having the right language skills.

Strict translation of words and terms will be unhelpful, therefore time needs to be spent on the interpretation of the interpretation. Systems theory and family therapy skills can be used right from the start of engaging with the family by:

- Enabling everyone to have their say.
- Circular questioning to enable expression of feelings.
- Reinforcing the integrity of the family system.
- Noting patterns of communication and structure.

Having established a helping relationship a systems perspective enables you to locate the family system within a wider system of agencies, resources and a local environment that is generally hostile. Your networking skills can mobilise the statutory agencies to provide what is required to attend to the immediate areas of concern and clarify roles and responsibilities. A case conference or network meeting can put this on a formal basis with an action check list for future reference to monitor the plan. One option may be to plan some family sessions together with a colleague from another agency such as social work, health or education. This could combine assessment and intervention work to ascertain medium term needs whilst using family therapy skills to help the family establish their equilibrium. The key is to enable them to re-establish *their* particular coping mechanisms and ways of dealing with stress, rather than trying to impose an artificial solution. Maintaining a systems-wide perspective can help you evaluate the factors and elements building up to form a contemporary picture of their context. Working with them as a family and demonstrating simple things like reliability and consistency will provide them with an emotional anchor, a secure enough base to begin to manage themselves in due course.

Elements of socially inclusive practice

Practitioners have to assess needs, evaluate risks and allocate resources in a way that is equitable as far as possible for a wide range of service users in various situations (Walker, 2003). Challenging oppression in relation to key issues such as poverty and social marginalisation that underpin interactions in social welfare, requires a holistic approach to social change that tackles oppression at the personal, institutional and cultural levels (Dominelli, 2002). An empowering practice can contribute to the defence of marginalised people using an overarching systems framework. A review of the elements that constitute a socially inclusive practice lists four core intervention skills necessary to build on an authentic practice that reflects your humanitarian values (Smale et al., 2000):

- Social entrepreneurship.
- Reflection.
- Challenging.
- Reframing.

These elements have a lot in common with family therapy approaches. **Social entrepreneurship** is the ability to initiate, lead and carry through problem-solving strategies in collaboration with other people in all kinds of social networks. **Reflection** is the worker's ability to pattern or make sense of information, in whatever form, including the impact of their own behaviour and that of the organisation on others. **Challenging** refers to the ability of staff to confront people effectively with their responsibilities, their problem-perpetuating or creating behaviours and their conflicting interests. **Reframing** is the worker's ability to help redefine circumstances in ways which lead towards problem resolution.

Practitioners must counteract oppression, mobilise users' rights and promote choice, yet have to act within organisational and legal structures which users experience as oppressive (Braye and Preston-Shoot, 1997). Finding your way through this dilemma and reaching compromises, or discovering the potential for creative thinking and practice, are the challenges and opportunities open to practitioners committed to a socially inclusive practice. This means treating people as wholes, and as being in interaction with their environment, of respecting their understanding and interpretation of their experience, and seeing clients at the centre of what workers are doing (Payne, 1997). The unique psycho-social perspective offers a vast reservoir of knowledge and skills to bring to bear on the multiple problems of socially excluded people. Systems theory and practice ensures that the effort put in is more likely to address every possible dimension and be more effective. Figure 5.1 illustrates the multiple systems potentially impacting on a particular family.

Anti-racist and anti-oppressive practice is repeatedly referred to in the caring literature and they have a long historical lineage as part of the social justice basis of modern practice. The concepts are backed up in codes of conduct, ethical guidance and occupational standards defined by central and local government, requiring services to meet the needs of diverse cultures and combat discrimination. They are part and parcel of what attracts many of us into helping in the first place. Translating good intentions into daily practice is, however, harder than it might at first appear.

For example, in the case of child care practice, there is still a tendency for practitioners to proceed with assessment on the basis that the mother is the main responsible carer, with the father taking a minor role. Women are perceived therefore as responsible for any problems with their children and for their protection. You may feel that this reflects the reality, especially in cases of single parenthood, or domestic violence, where fathers are absent or a threat. Anti-oppressive practice requires in these situations acknowledgement of the mother's predicament and multiple dilemmas. It requires an informed practice using feminist and systems theory to evaluate the situation and seek every small opportunity to support the mother and engage the father. The combination of personal guilt felt by women in these circumstances, with a mother-blaming tendency in society can erode their precarious coping skills and paradoxically, increase child protection risk factors. Family therapy skills in a non-blaming context can help.

A history of childhood mental health problems is strongly indicated in the risk factors for developing adult mental health problems. It is imperative therefore that the needs of all black and ethnic minority children vulnerable to mental health problems are addressed early and competently in order to prevent later problems. Your anti-racist work in multi-disciplinary ways as part of inter-agency groups co-ordinating efforts to support the child and family through temporary or moderate difficulties could be critical. As a practitioner using systems theory you can support other staff in statutory or voluntary resources by offering a more holistic evaluation and assessment of the family process adapted to take account of cultural diversity.

One of the central aims of anti-racist and anti-oppressive practice is to exclude the risk of misinterpretation or underplaying significant emotional and behavioural characteristics in black families. An understanding of the reluctance and resistance of black parents to consider a mental health explanation for their child's behaviour or emotional state is important when considering how to engage parents or carers from diverse cultural backgrounds in the process of support

(Walker, 2003). It is equally important to make efforts to understand cultural explanations and belief systems around disturbed behaviour as part of risk assessment work. Respecting rather than challenging difference should be the starting point for finding ways of moving forward in partnership and co-operation. The dilemma in aspiring to practice in anti-oppressive ways is in balancing this respect with knowledge and evidence of the consequences of untreated emerging mental health problems.

The characteristics of non-Western societies such as collectivism, community and physical explanations for emotional problems are in contrast to Western concepts of individualism and psychological explanations (Bochner, 1994). The Western model of mental illness ignores the religious or spiritual aspects of the culture in which it is based. However, Eastern, African and Native American cultures tend to integrate them (Fernando, 2002). Spirituality and Religion can be critical components of a family's well being, offering a source of strength and hope in trying circumstances. You need to address this dimension as part of the constellation of factors affecting black families, avoiding stereotyping, and bearing in mind the positive and sometimes negative impact spiritual or religious beliefs might have on their mental health.

Basing your practice on anti-oppressive principles is not a soft option; it is not just signing up to political correctness, or about being nice to black people. It is about how you define yourself as a practitioner and your relationship to service users. A recent powerful contribution to the literature on this issue makes the point that you cannot bolt-on a bit of anti-oppressive practice, it has to be part and parcel of all your everyday practice, as a contribution to tackling poverty, social justice, and the structural causes of inequality (Dominelli, 2002). This goes against theories of practice that advocate a maintenance or care management role for practitioners. Wherever you position yourself you will probably find yourself occupying different roles at different times in your work regardless of your explicit intentions. This is because if you are client-centred then you will engage with them in partnership to help meet their needs to maintain them in their current circumstances, provide therapeutic input or offer care management if that is what families want. All of these approaches and the tasks within them can be informed by family therapy skills and systems theory.

CHAPTER 6

Attachment Theory and Family Therapy

Introduction

There is a tendency in present thinking to believe we can 'deal' with our past and move on. To some extent clearly we can but there is always more that can surprisingly disturb as the future unfolds through new life events. Attachments from the past remain powerful and form the basis of future relationships. In this chapter the interplay between ideas from **attachment theory** (which is largely concerned with dyadic relationships) and **family systems theory** (concerned with the whole family) will be explored.

John Bowlby, who is usually thought of in relation to attachment theory rather than family therapy, clearly saw attachment relationships and family life as intertwined:

Evidence is accumulating that human beings of all ages are happiest and able to deploy their talents to their best advantage when they are confident that, standing behind them, there are one or more trusted persons who will come to their aid should difficulties arise. The person trusted, also known as an attachment figure, can be considered as providing his (or her) companion with a secure base from which to operate.

(Bowlby, 1979).

A main aim of family therapy is to enable all members to relate together in such a way that each member can find a secure base in his relationships within the family, as occurs in every healthily functioning family. To this end attention is directed to understanding the ways in which family members may at times succeed in providing each other with a secure base but at other times fail to do so, by misconstruing each other's roles, by developing false expectations of each other, or by redirecting forms of behaviour that would be appropriately directed towards one family member towards another.

(Bowlby, 1979).

Since Bowlby described these concepts there has been enormous effort to understand the different types of attachment relationships and their significance for the individual. More recently attention has turned to how these relationships are played out in the drama of family life.

Attachment theory is currently very popular in child and family practice. It is included in government guidelines for practitioners assessing families (Bentovim and Bingley Miller, 2002) and as a tool for understanding a child's developmental experiences. Family systems theory and attachment theory share common origins: both developed in opposition to the limitations of psychoanalytic perspectives in the treatment of children or individuals, emphasised the importance of 'real' relationships and children's 'real' environments, and were influenced by general systems thinking. Attachment theory offers unique data about the **dyadic relationship**.

Being able to recognise the strategies children use within a dyadic relationship provides useful information about how the dyad has related in the past and helps clinicians formulate questions and hypothesis, and plan family interventions. Attachment patterns are observable. They do not require the infants or young children to articulate verbally their contribution to the relationship, but do require the child to relate to the parent as he or she always does, thus telling a story about the parent-child relationship. In other words in attending to the attachment relationship, clinicians take into account the young child's non-verbal story of their experiences in the child-carer context.
(Kozlowska and Hanney, 2002).

Similarly adult attachment categories can be invaluable when working with intergenerational and family origin issues. It provides a useful *schema* to explore the ongoing impact of past relationships and gives useful information about issues of unresolved loss or trauma. The main classifications used to describe child and adult attachments are summarised below.

Infant attachment classifications

The four established categories of infant attachment are:

1. Secure/B (the infant shows signs of missing the parent, seeks proximity on reunion, and then returns to play).
2. Avoidant/A (the infant ignores and avoids the parent on reunion).
3. Ambivalent/C (the infant is highly distressed and highly focussed on the parent, they cannot be settled by the parent and may seek proximity and display anger in quick succession).
4. Disorganised/D (the attachment figure is also a source of alarm and is unpredictable).

Adult attachment classifications

The original adult classifications are:

1. Secure/autonomous with respect to attachment (associated with the parents of secure/B infants).

2. Dismissive of attachment (associated with the parents of avoidant/A infants).
3. Preoccupied by past attachment relationships and experiences (associated with parents of ambivalent/C infants).

Adult attachment categorisations are derived not from the actual experiences of childhood attachment but from the way the person describes and currently interprets these childhood experiences. Thus it is possible to have had difficult or traumatic experiences as a child but as an adult to have come to some resolution of these. An adult in this situation would be categorised as autonomous and would be likely to have a secure attachment with their own child. An adult who had not resolved such experiences would be likely to have an insecure attachment with their own child (Main and Goldwyn, 1991). The link between 'inner' mental representation and 'outer' manifestation is of great interest to family therapy which is concerned with the balance between the needs of the family system and the needs of the individuals within it.

Integrating family systems theory and attachment theory

The question of how to develop these two theories, both of which are fundamentally focussed on family relationships and their impact on the individuals' development is taxing researchers. In terms of their relevance to practice the government and caring agencies are increasingly keen to standardise practitioner's assessments of children and families. The theoretical underpinnings are critical here, as standardising the collection of information is relatively simple but making sense of data requires complex theoretical frameworks. Children have different attachments to each of their parents so it is not possible to understand a family based on just one of these relationships. Similarly adult attachment security relates to specific relationships and may alter or develop over time. Recent research increasingly indicates that both child and adult categorisations are subject to change rather than remaining fixed (Cook, 2000; Feeney, 2003). Both the ideas from attachment theory and from family therapy are needed to aid practitioners in their assessment of a family.

There is considerable debate as to how these theoretical ideas might be combined or integrated. Three models are described below: the **Dynamic Maturational Model** which proposes expanding the attachment categories in a way which is helpful to modern practice with families; the **Network Model** which proposes keeping the ideas separate but valuing their differing contributions; and the **Family Attachment Measure** which proposes an integration in order to assess family attachment. All three models have useful contributions to further our understanding of family processes and the importance of attachment relationships. Some readers will prefer one approach to the others but all three are included as they have distinctive contributions to offer.

The Dynamic Maturational Model

Crittenden (1999) suggests that from a clinical perspective the normative A, B, C classifications are rarely found when working with disadvantaged, or traumatised populations. Crittenden's expanded classifications are helpful, for practitioners working with families, in emphasising the adaptations which people make to deal as best they can with the difficult circumstances they find themselves in. The **Dynamic Maturational Model** (DMM) emphasis the notions of adaptation, development and change. In contrast to other attachment models, which emphasise continuity of attachment classification, this model emphasises the dynamic interaction between maturation and experience.

In the DMM model all attachment strategies are seen as adaptations to a particular relationship. In other words children's behavioural and mental strategies are seen as organised and biologically determined, and function to increase the probability of safety and survival. The child's behaviour is understood as adaptive in the light of their relationships and other factors such as illness, loss or trauma. (This conceptual approach is similar to the family therapist technique of positive reframing.) In practice this is important because the model focuses on the strengths and strategies

that the child has developed rather than on weaknesses or deficits. It has an innate respect for the children and adults who have had to contend with difficult circumstances. It also conceptualises attachment strategies, or ways of relating to caregivers, as becoming more complex over the lifespan.

Although treatment or intervention is often informed by attachment data it may occur at the individual, dyadic, marital or family system level. Using attachment-derived data does not necessarily result in an 'attachment' intervention. Because of the connections between systems, interventions on family or marital levels can bring about change in the child's attachment relationships. This is compatible with the Network Model below, which takes information from different levels in the family system to inform interventions.

Endangered attachment strategies

Rather than using the 'disorganised' category for the 15 per cent of the normative population who do not fit the original ABC categorisations Crittenden has begun to differentiate this group into clinically more meaningful categories. These endangered attachment strategies are described in detail as they are particularly relevant to practitioners and as yet not widely available in the literature.

The endangered 'C's: C3-C4

As with the normative C, these parents are inconsistent in their response to the child. That is they are variously sensitive, caring and unresponsive. The key difference is that the parent's lack of response leaves the child either feeling unsafe or actually being unsafe. In reaction to this the child develops strategies that elicit parental attention even if this involves angry or risk taking behaviour. Anger involves threatening or aggressive behaviour such as hitting, kicking, swearing (C3), while disarming coy behaviour escalates to feigned helplessness (C4). Parents may engage with the behaviour e.g. angry, coercive battles, or ignore it. The latter may lead to escalating behaviour and risk taking such as running into the road, attempting suicide or becoming more helpless and unable to function.

The implications of such behaviours is that issues such as abuse, neglect, failure to supervise, use of punitive parenting techniques and factors underlying parental inconsistency, like drug and alcohol misuse, mental illness or other family relationship difficulty need to be clarified. Although apparently dysfunctional from an attachment perspective, the child's behaviour can be reframed as adaptive in view of the family's past context, and having functioned to ensure parental proximity and involvement. Such reframing helps move the blame away from the child or family and gives the family the opportunity to find new ways of relating to meet the child's needs for consistency and protection from attachment figures.

The endangered 'A's: A3-A4

For non-normative A's the danger may lie in extreme parental withdrawal, hostility, anger, displeasure or acceptance of the child being dependent on compliance or performance. Parents of endangered As consistently punish demonstrations of negative affects (e.g. desire for comfort, distress or anger) with further withdrawal, anger or rejection of the attachment behaviour or the child. While endangered Cs exaggerate negative affect to ensure parental interaction, endangered As improve their interaction with their caregivers by inhibiting negative affect or by displaying false negative affect.

Compulsively caregiving children (A3) work hard to maintain a relationship with a vulnerable, depressed or withdrawn attachment figure that has retreated too far and requires care from the child. Assessment of these families must include consideration of parenting capacity, parental psychopathology, physical illness and availability of other supports that can improve parental function.

Compulsively compliant (A4) attachment relationships are characterised by 'good' children. These children inhibit negative affect and focus intensely on tasks and on getting them right. Parents are likely to become angry or dismissive of practitioners who try to explore relationship issues. The only avenue for a child to express

distress or anger in a safe way may be illness or physical symptoms. By being ill the child maintains the appearance of compliance, and simultaneously elicits care and protection.

Understanding the A4 strategy enables practitioners to plan interventions carefully, in a way which avoids confrontation, which could compromise the child and result in outright rejection of the therapeutic process by the parents.

Crittenden's model, and in particular the extended attachment categories, offer new ways of thinking about some of the attachment behaviour observed in families with relationships under stress and can be easily incorporated into some of the family assessment strategies described in earlier chapters. All of the ideas put forward by the attachment theorists require practitioners to develop their skills in observation of young children and offer further ways to interpret such observations.

The Network Model

The **Network Model** (NM) (Capra, 1997) refers to the application of general systems theory to living systems. A key characteristic of living systems is the tendency to form multi-levelled structures of systems within systems. Although each system remains distinct, it is simultaneously part of a more complex system that is distinct in its own right. Inherent in the Network Model is the understanding that although the information from different levels of complexity is unique, it is neither more nor less fundamental than information from another level.

With this model integration of family and attachment theories implies the ability to recognise each level of complexity as distinct yet interconnected. Using the Network Model, the integration of attachment and family systems theories does not mean either merging them or keeping them distinct. Rather, integration refers to the ability to recognise each level of complexity (e.g. dyad versus family) as distinct yet interconnected, and it enables our attention to move through different 'levels of complexity' as required. Figure 6.1 illustrates this complexity.

This NM therefore means that the practitioner is able to consider the unique properties of a

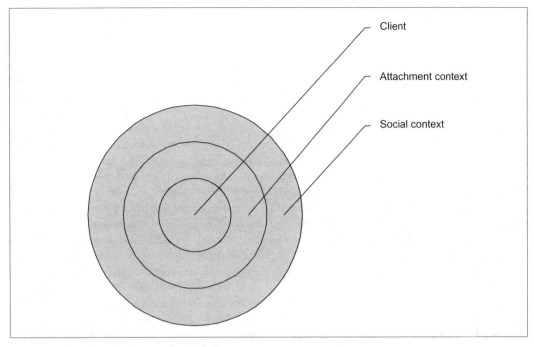

Figure 6.1: Complexity in the network model

dyadic relationship, together with the unique properties of the family system, as well as the relationship between them. This is essentially a simple model but vital in practice: it is easy for the complexities of family relationships to become impossible to disentangle and this offers a way to separate key components. For example, it may be that one of the attachment relationships in a family is key to the problems being experienced by the whole family. In this situation the intervention will need to pay attention to the specific dyadic relationship as well as the family system.

The Family Attachment Measure

In contrast to the Network Model the **Family Attachment Measure** (FAM) is based on a proposed integration of attachment and systemic theories as a way of assessing family attachment. The approach argues that the key elements of attachment processes are affect regulation, interpersonal understanding, information processing and the provision of comfort within intimate relationships. They see these as equally applicable

to family processes provided that: attachment processes at the individual level are linked to family processes using the shared frames or representations of emotions, cognitions and behaviour; that there is explicit consideration of the nature and quality of the dynamic between attachment and other processes in family life; that there is a conceptualisation of the relationship between individual and family processes (Hill et al., 2003).

The FAM is an adaptation of the **Adult Attachment Interview** given to the family group in which members are asked to consider questions about relationships and a range of safety, discipline and attachment issues in the present. Taking attachment theory as the starting point the authors describe how although the research has taken an overwhelmingly individual perspective, attachment theory is concerned with the implication of relational processes for individuals (Hill et al., 2003). The details of the FAM interview as outlined are not yet in press. The idea of integration of these two key theories is attractive. The authors are correct to highlight the fact that the classical measure of attachment (the Strange Situation Test) looking at the interaction process between mother-infant dyads has always been systemic, but in view of the difficulties experienced by researchers in operationalising the Adult Attachment Interview we will have to await further publications to understand the place for the FAM interview.

Nonetheless this theoretical proposition is important in again taking steps to incorporate the ideas from attachment theory into family systems theory, in this case by integrating the two theoretical positions. All this adds up to a critical period in the development of the processes for understanding family life. The three models described above all contribute to our ways of assessing and interpreting the dyadic relationships which exist within the family and which have previously tended to be studied in separate domains.

Adult attachment, dating and marital relationships

A pivotal dyadic relationship in the family is the **marital relationship**. There has been substantial research into these relationships from the attachment perspective, looking back to each adult's attachment relationships with their own parents and forward to their couple relationship. In terms of child and family practice it is useful to review some of the recent research findings in this field as many decisions revolve around assessments of a couple's parenting capacity and of their capacity to change. Sometimes the arrival of children in a new couple relationship can cause great difficulties. Thus within the family context the ideas from adult attachment research, including that on dating relationships, can play a useful part in these assessments.

Hazan and Shaver (1987) proposed that romantic love is an attachment process. They were concerned to create a 'coherent framework for understanding love, loneliness and grief at different points in the life cycle'. They considered that attachment theory could provide such a framework and also explain how both healthy and unhealthy forms of love originate as reasonable adaptations to specific social circumstances. Hazan and Shaver felt that the evidence of

continuity from adult/child studies of attachment (e.g. Main et al., 1985) added plausibility to the notion that a person's adult style of romantic attachment is also affected by attachment history.

Their research supported the idea of three different **love styles** rather than three points along a love continuum. However they cautioned that the degree of security in a relationship is a joint function of attachment style and factors unique to the particular partners and circumstances; and that they had probably overemphasised the degree to which attachment style and attachment-related feelings are traits rather than products of unique person-situation interactions. Attachment researchers often vacillate between using the terms secure, avoidant and anxious/ambivalent to describe relationships and using them to categorise people. We have focussed here on personal continuity, but we do not wish to deny that relationships are complex, powerful phenomena with causal effects beyond those predictable from personality variables alone (Hazan and Shaver, 1987).

The question of continuity and change in attachment style is also raised in this paper:

> It would seem overly pessimistic – from the perspective of insecurely attached people – to conclude that continuity is the rule rather than the exception between early childhood and adulthood . . . It seems likely that continuity between childhood and adult experiences decreases as one gets further into adulthood.
>
> (Hazan and Shaver, 1987).

There has been ongoing debate as to whether attachment style is a characteristic of the individual or of a specific relationship. Partners' characteristics can either maintain existing working models or promote change for better or worse (Feeney, 2003; Cook, 2001). Using data from a study of dating couples Feeney illustrates four key points:

1. The couple relationship can either foster or erode the sense of security of its members.
2. Pursuer-distancer cycles are especially relevant to an understanding of couples' attachment relationships.

3. Transition points provide a particular challenge for the couple system, as partners seek to re-establish familiar interaction patterns or to develop new patterns.
4. There is mutual influence between the couple unit and other subsystems of the family.

(Feeney, 2003).

Feeney concludes that attachment theory has a particular strength in addressing the emotions and motivations associated with intimate relating, whereas systems theory highlights the need to consider the broader context in which individuals and relationships are embedded. Systems theory emphasises transition points, notably the different stages in the life cycle of the family, as times when families are more likely to experience distress. For example, the transition from being a family with young children to that of a family with adolescents often puts stress on the family; having to adapt to the changing developmental needs of the teenagers at the same time can impact on the couple's own relationship.

A systemic theoretical model

What is the contribution of adult attachment styles to dating and marital relationships? The sense of attachment security is associated with:

- Positive beliefs about couple relationships.
- The formation of more stable couple relationships.
- Satisfaction with dating relationships and marriage.
- High levels of intimacy, commitment and emotional involvement within the relationship.
- Positive patterns of communication.

Using a systemic model the changes in any aspect of the system affect other parts of the system. Attachment insecurity in one member is likely to have ripple effects through the whole system. These dynamics mean that changes which occur in one part of the system, (e.g. parent/child relationship), can alter some aspect of the association between secure attachment and couple relationship quality.

Extension to the wider family system

A growing body of research finds concordance between mothers' adult attachment and their attachment relationship with their child. It has been widely assumed that quality of the parent/child relationship is the linking mechanism – that adults who are securely attached themselves tend to provide a secure base for their children (Byng-Hall, 1998). It is also being suggested that the relationship between the parents plays a central role in the generational transmission of working models of attachment; that marital quality may play a causal role in affecting parenting style and children's adaptation. In other words, that the family system plays a part as well as the dyadic parent/child relationship.

Extrapolating from these findings, and subject to replication and extension of the results, we conclude that the transmission of attachment relationships from grandparents to parents to children is not simply a matter of parenting. When a person learns early on that he or she is worthy of love, and that adults will be responsive and available in times of need, he or she is more likely to establish satisfying relationships with other partners, and to have the inclination and ability to work toward solving relationship problems and regulating emotions so that they do not escalate out of control.

(Mikulincer et al., 2002).

This leads to the place for family therapy in working with families, not only on problems which are clearly involving the whole family but also where problems arise in dyadic relationships. It also raises the question of how to help adults move on and restructure their adult attachment, where this is part of the problem.

Restructuring adult attachment

One intervention targeting adult attachments is **Emotionally Focussed Couples Therapy** (EFT). EFT is a therapy which enables couples to redefine and repair their attachment bond (Johnson and Best, 2003). Habitual attachment responses are viewed as strategies that are influenced by the patterns of interaction in particular relationships. While not proposing to describe the details of this particular model, it is significant in the capability of attachment style being altered through the therapeutic process. Research suggests that a significant percentage of people do change their attachment style, or ways of engaging others, over time.

> *Negative attachment-related events, particularly abandonments and betrayals, can cause seemingly irreparable damage to close relationships. Many partners enter therapy not only in general distress but also with the goal of bringing closure to such events, thus restoring lost intimacy and trust. During the therapy process, however, these events, which we have termed attachment injuries, often re-emerge in an alive and intensely emotional manner, much like a traumatic flashback, and overwhelm the injured partner.*
>
> (Johnson et al., 2001).

The concept of an attachment injury does not focus so much on the specific content of a painful event but on the attachment significance of such events. The attachment injury occurs when one partner fails to respond to the expectation of comfort and caring in times of danger or distress. The incident may then become a recurring theme and creates an impasse that blocks relationship repair in the couple's therapy. This may help to explain why some couples have difficulty responding to therapy and offers a different lens to be used to view the components of the change process.

The couple as an attachment partnership

The concepts of the couple as an **attachment partnership**, and of the interactive nature of the individuals' internal working models of relationships in the specific relationship, offer a unique way of viewing couple relationships. It also enables an understanding of change and development within those relationships. Some studies have looked at how differing adult attachment styles may lead to effective or ineffective caregiving within the relationship and also suggest

mediating mechanisms such as **social support knowledge** and **prosocial orientation** (Feeney and Collins, 2001).

Others have looked at specific relationship issues such as Morrison et al. (1997) who found respondents with avoidant or ambivalent attachment described more hostility in their relationships than secure participants. Scott and Cordova (2002) looked at whether attachment styles moderated the relationship between marital adjustment and depressive symptoms among husbands and wives. Their findings suggest a relationship between insecurity and a predisposition to depressive symptoms in marital relationships. Cohn et al. (1992) found that husbands classified as secure showed more positive interactions with their wives than insecure husbands.

These studies give some indication of the usefulness of considering couples' relationships from both the systemic and attachment perspectives. They also show how the components of family assessment can be used together to plan appropriate interventions with families. Ignoring the attachment status of family members runs the risk of designing interventions which at best will fail the family and at worst may prove detrimental. If we look at the frameworks for family assessment suggested, for practitioners, by the government, much of the data needed for these processes is still being collected; the art is to use that data within the conceptual frameworks from which they have been abstracted.

The family as an attachment system

What kind of events threatens relationships? A brief look at jealousy gives a window into some of the potential impacts of life cycle changes in the family. One suggestion is that romantic jealousy is consistent with the idea that jealousy is in part, the product of threats to attachment relationships. In jealousy-provoking situations, people react not only to the possible loss of a romantic partner but also to the possible loss of an attachment figure (Sharpsteen and Kirkpatrick, 1997).

Jealousy is clearly often construed in relation to threats or 'attachment injuries' from a real or perceived adult competitor. Not insignificant however are the experiences of jealousy in relation to one's own offspring. The often much-longed-for child arrives and disrupts the patterns of the couple's relationship. The system has to alter to accommodate the new member; and the couple's attachment relationship will need to accommodate their both having new attachments to their child. Rivalry is a dynamic that has always been talked about in relation to all interfamily relationships, from Freud's intergenerational rivalry through to romantic jealousy and sibling rivalry (Dunn, 1995).

Mikulincer and Florian (1999) looked at the relation between spouses' self-reports of attachment style and their perceptions of family dynamics in parents of small children. During this stage of family development, the initial dyadic relationship is transformed into a more complex pattern of familial interaction, which should be examined from the family dynamic perspective. The analysis of ideal representations of family dynamics showed that what people, differing in attachment styles, reveal in their perception of family cohesion fits the intimacy level they ideally want within the family. So that secure and anxious-ambivalent persons' family interactions seem to be guided by intimacy-related goals, whereas avoidant persons' family relationships seem to be guided by distance goals.

These findings suggest ways to take adult attachment theory into account as well as systemic theory.

For example, when familial conflicts emerge around the theme of cohesiveness, the therapist should also consider the possibility of goal incongruency, in addition to a search for emotional inhibitions and interpersonal skills deficiencies. Therapeutic resources can be invested in the clarification of each spouses' 'hidden agenda' regarding intimacy in the relationship. However, when family distress evolves from lack of family adaptability, the therapist may focus on interpersonal deficiencies, related emotional inhibitions, and defensive processes.

(Mikulincer and Florian, 1999).

These findings concur with the concepts discussed earlier in this chapter of the interrelationship between attachment style and the actors involved in the partnership.

There have been enormous steps in the last five years in looking at the interactions between attachment and systemic theoretical basis. The contribution to understanding the dilemmas faced, by individuals, throughout the life-cycle by the two theories is well established. That attachment style can develop and may change throughout an individual's life, in the context of their experiences in relationships, enhances the understanding of family systems (e.g. Mikulincer et al., 2002). The work on romantic relationships and attachment strategies (e.g. Hazan and Shaver, 1987) forms the platform to begin to understand the processes involved in moving from being a couple to a family with three or more members (e.g. Mikulincer and Florian, 1999).

Overall there is wide support, in the research findings, for practitioners working with either individuals or families to pay close attention to the attachment styles and relationships (dyadic) within the family as well as working with the whole family system. The duality of approach enables a more detailed understanding of the family dynamics. Utilising the concepts embodied in the network model also supports the practice of combining family and individual therapies as appropriate. While there is still a long way to go it is clear that thinking about the family system alone or about the attachment dyad alone is limiting, and we should try to consider both paradigms.

This is easy to say, and hard to do. How to work with attachments is unclear. Family therapy offers clear ways of working with a family and can include work focussed on dyadic relationships which may alter attachments. The family therapist has to consider the place for individual, couple and whole family interventions, and their potential impact on the attachment relationships.

CHAPTER 7

Families and Social Policy

Introduction

If one of the defining characteristics of a family therapy approach to your work is the need to take account of the wider socio-economic context of family experience, then it is equally necessary to broaden your organisational frame of reference. This will enable you to take account of the influences on your practice of social policies and the economic and political agenda of the early twenty-first century. The key purpose of social work has been defined as:

> *A profession which promotes social change, problem solving in human relationships and the empowerment and liberation of people to enhance well being. Utilising theories of human behaviour and social systems, social work intervenes at the points where people interact with their environments. Principles of human rights and social justice are fundamental to social work.*
> (In: BASW, 2002).

This powerful statement from a representative body of practitioners from around the globe states quite clearly the twin elements that enshrine modern child and family practice – the relationship between the external social world, and the inner psychological experience of the individual that cause some citizens pain and suffering. In order to better understand how to help in these situations practitioners need to develop the capacity to undertake assessments and interventions in a wide variety of settings with individuals, families, and groups. The enlargement of the European Union poses challenges for those involved in the task of defining social policy and practice across national boundaries. Caring work is still linked to national policies, legislation, and cultural traditions that cannot be characterised as homogeneous, but which all in some way or another try to support families. Nevertheless there is a public perception that while closer economic integration could undermine national sovereignty, so there is a professional perception that closer social integration could threaten practitioner autonomy. This makes the task of identifying best practice and designing appropriate family support policies and practice across Europe, a challenging one.

Many European models of social welfare imply a residual role for the state and have a history of Church, charitable and non-governmental provision. Almost the reverse can be observed in the development of the British welfare state, until recently. Contemporary social policy initiatives and government statements confirm a re-definition of the welfare state whereby a larger role for the voluntary and independent social care sector is prescribed. In essence, family support and preventive work is being excluded from the remit of professional staff whose role is being more narrowly defined in assessment and care management terms. A combination of economic circumstances and sociological changes in people's behaviour has prompted social policy makers to consider how to meet the needs of contemporary families. A long history of interest and concern by welfare policy makers influenced by studies of family life can be traced to recent evidence providing a developing picture of changing family characteristics. These have accelerated over the past thirty years across Europe (NCH Action for Children, 2000; Home Office *Social Trends*, 1997; DoH *General Household Survey*, 1997; Utting, 1995):

- Rising trend in divorce.
- Increase in single parent households and cohabitation.
- Structural change in the pattern of family relationships.
- The widening gap between rich and poor.
- Increased numbers of mothers in work.
- The ageing of the population.
- Rise in youth homelessness.
- Increased reporting of domestic violence.
- Child and adolescent mental health problems.
- Increased alcohol and substance misuse.

Racism and xenophobia have increased as European Union enlargement has accelerated migration; armed conflict has precipitated increased numbers of asylum seekers; and economic and social dislocation has prompted more refugee applications to wealthier member countries. Families have been shattered and scattered, often in traumatic and extremely distressing circumstances. These changes in the socio-geographic texture of Europe have produced moral panics, and hasty policy changes to tackle the symptoms and consequences, without much thought put into understanding the causes. The emphasis seems to be on dealing with large population movements as a political and economic problem, rather than as a social issue about the welfare of children and families.

Practitioners know only too well the value and cost-effectiveness of early intervention and preventive work with families in trouble. There has always been an interest among caring professionals in providing earlier and more appropriate support to families where help with children and young people is needed. This could be in order to prevent more serious problems developing, or to deflect the need for statutory intervention (Baradon et al., 1999; Gardner, 1998; Gibbons and Wilding, 1995; Iwaniec, 1995). The need for a response from European practitioners is evident.

Family support in Britain has tended to attract much less attention in terms of government policy emphasis or research and development, than the more clearly defined systems for children in need of statutory protection and those looked after by local authorities. Yet it is covered by the same legal requirement of the Children Act 1989, and underpinned by the 1989 UN Convention on the Rights of the Child. The Department of Health refocussing children's services initiative (1995) together with the *Quality Protects* programme (1999), and new *Assessment Guidance* (2000), are all evidence of a policy shift designed to influence practice, prompted by research into family support services and the limitations of the child protection system (Thoburn et al., 1998; DoH, 1995).

Within these broad focus findings, detailed studies have detected intra-familial changes in traditional patterns of kinship relationships and contact and support, where significant numbers of families have lost touch or were unable to rely on help when it was needed. These findings are of enormous interest to practitioners seeking to intervene therapeutically while harnessing the natural network of support preferable to many people (Speak et al., 1995; Coleman et al., 1997; McGlone et al., 1998). Further complexity is revealed by research into sub-groups of the population which although sparse, offers evidence of the nature and variety of contemporary family life. For example, Modood and Berthoud (1997) found that while all ethnic groups had high levels of contact with non-resident parents, Asian and African-Caribbean people had higher levels of contact with aunts and uncles. The potential of other family members and grandparents as helpful resources is indicative of a need for the widening of the focus for practitioners expected to assess strengths within the existing family constellation and work preventively. A family therapy orientation can help make sense of all these variables affecting the relationships within families.

The diverse nature of family life in contemporary Britain and in other European societies therefore requires sophisticated analysis of the broad trends reported in social surveys, otherwise abrupt policy changes can fail to address fully the needs of every family requiring support. Racist and cultural stereotypes of the role played by extended families distort the picture of unique family situations which are complex and fluid, and inhibit proper assessment of the needs of black and other ethnic minority families, travellers, and refugee families. These families all face additional problems in the context of prejudice, institutional racism and discrimination, which can find expression in child care and adult mental health problems where family therapy can offer help (Dominelli, 1999; Kiddle, 1999; Vostanis and Cumella, 1999).

Service design and delivery

It is crucial for the future development of family life that support services are designed and delivered in the most effective and accessible way possible. Staff require an understanding of the different cultures and professional knowledge and theories used by other staff in different agencies in order to integrate and co-ordinate help for children and families. Services geared towards the needs of specific age groups of children or young people, or adults can determine the type of help offered and whether it is perceived as family or individual support. This becomes particularly important in the area of child and family work where the initial assessment of the presenting problem could be formulated on an individual or family basis. Practitioners trained in family therapy are particularly alert to the potential for scapegoating individual children or adults within family systems functioning in negative and punitive ways (Dallos and Draper, 2000).

Assessment methodology designed around the needs of bureaucratic systems intent on rationing and restricting access to support services in this context tends to remain rooted in individualistic psychiatric diagnostic models. Psycho-social factors are embraced as risk factors reflecting negative, deficit indicators, rather than a more holistic systems theory approach seeking to identify and amplify strengths, coping strategies, alternative community resources, and user perceptions. Handled carefully assessment itself can be an empowering experience for service users embedded in a culture of blame and fault.

It has been established that a confluence of several risk factors in childhood can create the conditions for later psycho-social difficulty, including socio-economic disadvantage, child abuse, and parental mental illness. But there are protective mechanisms that can mitigate the chance of some children going on to develop anti-social behaviour or serious mental health problems. These can be obscured by the imperative for medical diagnosis or the over-reactions of inexperienced professionals or untrained volunteer family support workers.

The assessment of risk and resilience factors has been well documented in the literature (Rutter, 1985; Taylor and Devine, 1993; Howe et al., 1999; Parton, 1999). These include:

- The child's response to stress being determined by the capacity to appraise and attach meaning to their situation.
- Age-related susceptibilities which permit older children to use their greater understanding compared to younger children.
- How a child deals with adversity either actively or reactively and the ability to act positively, is a function of self-esteem and feelings of self-efficacy rather than of any inherent problem-solving skills.

This highlights the importance of assessment methods, informed by systems theory, that take account of not just individual characteristics within the child but equally within the family and broader environment. A social model of Europe incorporating the European heritage of social action in child and family practice could enlarge the panorama of assessment activity. In combination, a sophisticated assessment process using systems theory identifying strengths and protective factors, together with a more explicit social mandate, could create a chain of indirect links that foster improved family functioning in a context of social inclusion.

Organising services across the spectrum of multi-agency provision in partnership between different professionals and parents, offers the opportunity to bring out dormant protective factors to interrupt the causal chain of events so often set in train under retrenched child protection work (Little and Mount, 1999). A positive environment which promotes children's emotional well-being is preferable to reacting to the consequences of neglect or abuse. The Mental Health Foundation's latest inquiry into child and adolescent mental health (1999), concluded that a cultural shift was required which prioritised family support with a universally acceptable service of non-stigmatising provision. This should be available from schools, family doctors, and other accessible venues in order to address the increasing trend of mental health problems in children and young people. Service-driven models of assessment for children and families are the product of a reactive system geared to responding to concerns relating to child protection, developmental harm, or disturbed symptoms within a deficit framework. This leads to a focus on risk analysis which can be experienced by parents as undermining, or psychiatric treatment which constructs the child as suffering an individual disease requiring individual treatment.

The literature on assessment, and current Department of Health guidance are nevertheless improving to emphasise multi-faceted assessment but this is still influenced by psychiatric classifications located in a medico-biological model, and psychotherapeutic concepts (DoH, 1999; Baradon et al., 1999). There is less emphasis on psycho-social factors, including the effects of poverty, racism, unemployment, social exclusion and poor housing. *The Framework for Assessment of Children in Need* has been criticised for failing to properly distinguish family support from child protection, with many agencies organising their child welfare service as child protection (Calder, 2004). There is, however, evidence of some fresh thinking in this area, where attempts to offer a more sophisticated model of assessment are being made, stressing the interactive quality of assessment variables and the need for enhanced interpretative and planning skills (Middleton, 1997; Milner and O'Byrne,1998; Walker and Beckett, 2004). The emphasis is on the need for analysing and weighing the information generated during the assessment process ensuring this is underpinned by partnership practice and service user involvement.

A number of themes emerge from the research literature that help to consider the context of family and children's difficulties. These include the importance of multi-factorial causal explanations and the contribution of structural variables to childhood problems articulated by several authors (Sutton, 1999; Rutter et al., 1994). These demonstrate the value of taking a wider systems view of the situation being assessed. The importance of variation in perception of children's behaviour depending on the theoretical model used, and the evidence on assessment methodology, are crucial in determining the course and type of support offered. The interplay of these factors and the beneficial effects of developing a synthesis of models of intervention suggest precise targeted responses to particular children's difficulties combined with an expansive approach addressing social issues affecting children and families (Hill, 1999). The different way children's behaviour is understood by the child, the parent or carer and the professionals who encounter the child, are important to acknowledge and incorporate in any care plan or supportive intervention. A systems framework has the capacity to hold these divergent concepts and practices, valuing the contribution each makes. Differences in perception can therefore be seen as explanatory potential rather than be implicitly conflictual.

Practitioners have the opportunity to employ communication and relationship skills in direct family support work, using family therapy skills which they traditionally find rewarding, and which service users find more acceptable than intrusive, investigative risk assessment. Your role in multi-agency assessment and planning becomes significant in this context where several perceptions can be expressed, based on diverse evidence and different levels of professional anxiety. Practitioners managing these processes with individuals or groups in planning meetings, case conferences, or case reviews, require advanced negotiation and decision-making skills that can be enhanced with a systems perspective.

Case illustration

Your care team has had a family referred where there have been concerns about all of the four children at different times over a period of years. The parents separated recently and this appears to have tipped the main carer over the edge; he is requesting the children be accommodated because he cannot cope. The children's mother has left home before on several occasions following periods of drug and alcohol abuse combined with engaging in other relationships outside the marital partnership. The children are aged between 4 and 12 and have been on and off the child protection register in the categories of neglect and emotional abuse. The family are familiar with social services contact and have experienced several practitioners in the course of their involvement. The father has now given up employment to look after his children but as they get older he is finding it harder to cope with their needs and behaviour which often appears out of control.

Commentary

One of the characteristics of a family therapy approach is to consider the overall context of the referral and to consider in what way this is part of a sequence or pattern of events that is a well-trodden path. An initial inspection of this referral permits the hypothesis that both the family and professional system are familiar, though neither may be comfortable with the pattern of relationships that have developed over time. This might seem obvious but it offers very important information for you to consider when planning how to respond. If you want to use systems theory and offer a different experience, then there is an opportunity to change the familiar comfortable pattern anticipated by all the people involved.

One of the aspects of previous contacts may have been a crisis intervention style response whereby resources were put in to help support the carer and prevent the children being accommodated.

Unfortunately this style of response perhaps solved short-term problems but has not helped in the long run. The provision of support may have further undermined the father's fragile coping skills so that eventually he does not believe he can manage. Seeing their father unable to cope may trigger further episodes of testing behaviour as the children panic, and perhaps further driving him to despair. A circular pattern can be seen to have formed and be perpetuated by the family and professional system.

Using family therapy skills you and a colleague within your team or from another key agency in health, social work or education could convene meetings at the family home to focus on distinguishing the strengths and resources within the family and parent set-up. This challenges the previous pattern of referral response and enables new possibilities to emerge. Gender issues can be articulated openly to explore the meaning to the father and the children of his full-time caring role, and the departure of their mother. Instead of taking control and undermining his parental authority a family therapy approach resists this position and carefully and slowly facilitates him to reach solutions or consider options previously negated.

Families and professionals will have established fixed beliefs and assumptions about the family and themselves. Convening meetings with other professionals is another opportunity to reframe the presenting referral and consider new options, such as offering marital work with the parents to focus on their intimate relationship rather than the children's behaviour. Instead of perceiving themselves as failed parents you can help to encourage the notion that their needs as a couple are being overlooked as the focus continues to remain on the children. This concept could be liberating for them, the children and the professional system.

Early intervention and prevention

In the government policy consultation paper *Supporting Families* (1999) the focus of attention emphasised better support and education for current and future parents as a preventive strategy. Key themes included the intention to improve advice and information to parents, and achieving a reduction in child poverty, while offering financial help for working parents. The policy argues that by strengthening adult relationships and targeting serious family problems, an impact could be made on priority areas such as children's learning, youth offending, teenage pregnancy, and domestic violence. These are all areas that could be enhanced by a family therapy approach that can appraise the inter-relationship between and within them.

Various initiatives aimed at children, young people and their families living in disadvantaged areas such as the Sure Start programme are evidence of the practical implementation of the implicit preventive aspects of this policy which are based on evidence of success from the USA *Head Start* scheme (Gross et al., 1995). This demonstrated long-term reductions in anti-social activity, marital problems, child abuse, adult mental health difficulties, and unemployment in later life, in a group of children who received the intervention, with a comparison of children who did not receive the intervention.

Quantifying the impact of preventive family support work is complex, and to achieve systematic results is expensive, therefore there is little in the way of evidence of long-term effectiveness in Britain or the rest of Europe. However, there are signs that while outcome measures from the Department of Health refocussing initiative projects were intangible, small-scale social action projects could evidence changes in relationships between parents and professionals, how to work in partnership, and how to engage positively with parents (Robbins, 1998). All of these contributed to supporting families better and was more user-focussed.

The lessons for practice are for emphasising empowering strategies, searching hard for creative solutions beyond narrow service-led resources, and refining relationship-building skills. This challenges the service management orthodoxy for short-term focussed assessments aimed at identifying risk and need according to a limited range of resources provided by other non-statutory agencies. It offers the opportunity to provide professionally qualified practitioners with more satisfying work over longer time periods, and service users the chance to feel respected, valued, contained, and supported in a consistent and reliable way. The prospect is for combining the best features of contemporary practice grounded in a solid psycho-social systems theoretical base.

Supporting parents

Parent education or training programmes have expanded in the face of exponential demand for help from parents, to deal with a range of child and adolescent difficulties, from toddler tantrums to suicide and drug and alcohol addiction. This form of intervention is popular and is now expected to be offered as part of a repertoire of contemporary family support measures. Studies of parent education programmes, while they are limited in number, show they can be an effective way of supporting families by improving behaviour in pre-adolescent children (Lloyd, 1999; Bourne, 1993; Miller and Prinz, 1990). They highlight the impact that group-based behaviourally-oriented programmes have in producing the biggest subsequent changes in children's behaviour and are perceived by parents as non-stigmatising. Programmes where both parents are involved, and which include individual work with children, are more likely to effect long-term changes.

However parent education programmes whilst enjoying a growth in popularity in Britain and other European countries, are generally not subject to rigorous evaluation (Pugh and Smith, 1996). Research shows that in a number of studies 50 per cent of parents continue to experience difficulties, and it is not clear to what extent changes are due to the format, the method of intervention, the group support or the practitioner's skills. High attrition rates from some programmes are attributed to practitioner variables such as their level of qualification and experience, and qualities such as warmth, enthusiasm, or flexibility (Barlow, 1998). It may also be the case that some programmes are inappropriate for parents lacking motivation or feeling compelled to attend under the pressure of child protection concerns.

Few British studies have used randomised controlled trials, and this inhibits identification of the most beneficial elements of a programme: because most provision is geared to rectifying problems in disadvantaged groups, the available research evidence reflects that bias. Those that have been conducted are, nevertheless, yielding important qualitative data from stakeholder's perspectives (Morrow, 1998; Ghate and Daniels, 1997). It is argued that the tendency for the managerialist preference for evaluating work on the basis of the three 'E's' (efficiency, effectiveness, economy) which reflects service managers' agenda for quantitative outcome measures is limited. These data need to be supplemented with the three 'P's' (partnership, pluralism, process) which better reflect professional principles seeking to incorporate service users perspectives (Powell and Lovelock, 1992). Further studies which pay attention to normative models of parenting in the community would counter this bias by identifying skills that lead to successful parenting, focussing on what went right, rather than what went wrong.

Anti-racist practice demands attention to the family life cycle of black and other ethnic minority families focussing on transitional points, strengths and acceptable support (Kemps, 1997; Bhui and Olajide, 1999). We use the term black here and elsewhere to mean all ethnic minority communities who are systematically subjected to personal and institutional discrimination and prejudice. The views of parents and children are largely absent from the research, particularly in families with lone parents, gay and lesbian parents, and step-parents. There is also very little systematic incorporation of culture and ethnicity as factors influencing parenting styles, on disability and the particular issues facing parents with disabled children who may have emotional and behavioural problems, and on gender influences within families and within professional groups. A systems approach offers a perspective that can incorporate and value every possible influence on family experience.

Families for whom parent education is unlikely to be a sufficient response to child management difficulties are those which feature maternal depression, socio-economic disadvantage and the social isolation of the mother. Extra-familial conflict combined with relationship problems, contribute to the problem severity and chronicity and therefore influence the ability to introduce change. While parental misperception of the deviance of their children's behaviour is a significant impediment to engaging in constructive family support the prospects for unqualified staff attempting to help without professional supervision, are further diminished (Macdonald and Roberts, 1995).

Parenting education or training programmes seem to be a response to a demand for a variety of support, including information, child development knowledge, and skills development in managing children of all ages. It is a role undertaken in practice in the context of other work, most likely general family assessments, or specific risk assessments, where concerns have reached the threshold of statutory intervention. The gap between the demand and provision is currently met in the voluntary and private sector that is absorbing more and more complex work with fewer qualified staff. Yet family therapy skills deployed early enough are ideally suited to provide appropriate family support based on systems theory and best practice evidence.

The renaissance of family support in Britain is currently perceived as an alternative to child protection, rather than part of a connected architecture of resources to be activated as different needs emerge. Therefore the policy to develop indirect voluntary provision of family support services in Britain can be better seen as a symptom of, rather than solution to, retrenchment in family support offered by professional practitioners. The literature on family support in Europe (Cannan et al., 1992; Shardlow and Payne, 1998; Adams et al., 2000) acknowledges the dilemmas in seeking a common professional identity and family support practice which can simultaneously value autonomy in each member country. The rising trend in child and family problems across an expanding Europe with greater social mobility will demand existing and new skills of professional qualified practitioners. The concern is that economic and political pressure to promote a renaissance of voluntary, non-statutory family support, will produce the greatest stress on those least equipped to cope, and therefore precipitate child protection crises leading to further retrenchment of professional work.

Family group conferences

One way that children's services can tilt the balance away from repressive child protection procedures and illustrate the pragmatic use of systems theory is reflected in the example of **family group conferences** (FGC).

Introduced some years ago and borrowing from New Zealand Maori traditional practices, they have challenged the orthodoxy in social services planning which places primacy on the professional practitioner's power, values and perceptions. The key idea in these conferences is that family meetings are convened where there are concerns about the welfare of a child or children. The family here is defined widely and extended family members are encouraged to participate. Their task is to create their own plan for the child of concern by assuming responsibility in deciding how to meet the needs of the child.

Thus the practitioner's role changes dramatically from an inspectorial or adversarial role largely prescribed by procedures and a restricted definition of their task, to one more consistent with the skills and knowledge of family therapy. In the context of family group conferences practitioners can emphasise communication, negotiation, mediation and facilitation skills that are better informed by a family therapy approach seeking to emphasise problem-solving and highlight the strengths within a family system. Clearly a therapeutic stance is required that means practitioners having to embrace the concept of partnership practice and resist the seductive simplicity of deciding what is best for children and their families.

At the heart of the family group conference is a re-definition of practice with children, young people and families. It puts into sharp focus a tangible example of the elusive and often ill-defined notion of empowering practice. It is a challenge to practice that is driven by a defensive culture, and to practitioners comforted by the ability to retreat into procedural safety when faced with complexity, uncertainty, and the normal swings and roundabouts of family life. On the other hand this approach fits with practitioners using a family therapy approach to their work.

The FGC model proposes limits to the intrusion of the professional planning model. It suggests the model should form the frame within which family decision making should take place, and that decision making should be carried out in whatever way is appropriate for each particular family (Morris and Tunnard, 1996).

Domestic violence and the abuse of children

Critics of family therapy refer to domestic violence and the abuse of children by men as examples of the way many families are organised by male abuse of power, which is not sufficiently incorporated into systems theory. The hidden nature of the abuse together with the impossible dilemmas faced by women attempting to protect themselves and their children mean that it is likely to be a factor affecting the interactions between family members. Practitioners have equally been criticised for doubly oppressing women who, whilst attempting to manage their dilemmas and contradictory feelings, find themselves accused of failing to protect their children. Various studies have over the years confirmed that there is an under-reporting of this crime, and that domestic violence occurs in 30–50 per cent of male–female relationships (Kelly, 1996).

Critics argue that family therapy therefore colludes with male abuse of power because in seeking for example to foster parental control over difficult children, the method is actually reinforcing patriarchal authority. Statutory child care practitioners are themselves in a bind having a primary duty to prioritise the safety of children whilst recognising the risks posed to women who are frightened to report domestic violence for fear of having their children removed. The child protection system and the criminal justice system reflect social policies that implicitly collude with violence against women and children, and deter both from testifying and providing evidence against male perpetrators.

Recent research has highlighted the serious physical, psychological and emotional consequences for children who witness or are unwittingly involved in domestic violence. In 90 per cent of recorded incidents the child or children were in the next room, and in 30 per cent children tried to intervene to protect their mother from assault (Hester et al., 2000). Students of systems theory thus face having to make sense of concepts of interactivity and circular process, while simultaneously recognising the inequality and structural privileges provided to men. A thorough understanding of this crucial variable in contemporary relationship dynamics is required therefore for practitioners seeking to incorporate family therapy into their work with families where domestic violence is likely to be a major, yet unacknowledged factor.

Fortunately there is a growing body of literature that offers reliable evidence to employ in seeking to intervene in a thoughtful, ethical and empowering way for the *victims* as well as the *perpetrators* of domestic violence (Home Office, 2000; Hague, 2000; Walker, 2001b). Apart from direct work with a family where there is a suspicion but no open acknowledgement of domestic violence, systems theory can be put into practice within an inter-agency context. Well co-ordinated multi-agency collaboration has the potential to improve services to women and children experiencing domestic violence and to maximise their continual safety and well-being (Hester et al., 2000). Using a systems framework permits an understanding of the inter-agency relationships, rivalries, and different power positions that are played out in attempts at partnership practice.

User-friendly family therapy

The notion of **user-friendly family therapy** was coined by two family therapists who had, by the early 1990s become concerned about the technocratic feel of contemporary family therapy practice and who felt that family therapists were in danger of alienating families in need (Reimers and Treacher, 1995). Their thesis was that despite a tradition of agnosticism towards conventional psychiatry, individual treatments, and much orthodox thinking, family therapy as a movement had not fully embraced the more radical ideas of service user empowerment. Indeed they went as far as to quote from a classic social work text to offer a salutary warning of the dangers in ignoring

the views of the beneficiaries of helping interventions (Mayer and Timms, 1970).

Here is a good example of how social work principles and values can be added to the theoretical knowledge base of family therapy practice in order to strengthen it. This problem is not unique to family therapy and in terms of commitment to equal opportunities and anti-discriminatory practice family therapists are probably more enlightened than most in the therapeutic milieu. Generally speaking the aversion to user-involvement or the lack of research studies focussing on the user experience is reflected throughout the medical and therapeutic professions. This represents several issues that have been summarised thus (Rogers et al., 1993):

- Professionals feel entitled to disregard users' views when they do not coincide with their own.
- Psychiatric users are viewed as continually irrational and hence incapable of giving a valid view.
- Patients and relatives are assumed to share the same interests, and where they do not, the views of the former are disregarded by researchers.
- Professionals give partial credence to the clients' perspectives provided they fit in with their expert view.

Some of the elements of a user-friendly family therapy practice will resonate with practitioners who take an empowering anti-bureaucratic stance to their work and resist the pressure to squeeze service users into compartmentalised, managerialist processes that fail to address the needs and aspirations of vulnerable children and families. This sample illustrates the potential for synchronising the best practices of both social work and family therapy to the benefit of clients:

- *Ethical issues are of primary importance and the power difference between worker and user must be recognised as a major source of difficulty and danger.*
- *The building of a therapeutic alliance between users and therapists is usually crucial both to the success of therapy and the users reported satisfaction with therapy.*

■ *Successful therapy is at least partly dependent on the therapist discharging their responsibility to create a context which facilitates change.*

■ *User-friendly therapy recognises that therapists generally fail to understand the stress and distress that users experience.*

■ *Family members should be treated as unique individuals rather than as identical members of a family system, so that differences can be taken into consideration if successful therapy is to be undertaken.*

■ *Therapists must adopt a stance of self-reflexivity and thus if they themselves had difficulties, be willing to attend therapy sessions organised by therapists using a family therapy model similar to their own.*

(Reimers and Teacher, 1995)

Multi-disciplinary and inter-professional working

In recent years the volume and complexity of child and adolescent mental health problems has increased, rapidly prompting demands for help from parents, carers, and professionals. Subsequent public health enquiries and other research have highlighted the need for a collaborative response as existing provision has stretched beyond its capacity to cope adequately (Rutter et al., 1994; Rutter and Smith, 1995; Health Advisory Service, 1995; Harrington, 1997; Mental Health Foundation 1999; Rawlinson and Williams, 2000). Government policy directives encourage multi-disciplinary and more inter-professional working methods as part of the strategic response (House of Commons, 1997; Audit Commission, 1999; Walker, 1999). The creation of Children's Trusts will symbolically represent structural attempts to better co-ordinate services and meet the needs of children. The implications for practice with families highlights the need to find effective ways of working that avoid blaming, inter-agency scapegoating and placing further stress on families. The short term nature of family therapy combined with its systems perspective offers considerable advantages in this context.

One of the difficulties highlighted in a seminal piece of research was the gap which had been steadily growing for decades between the primary care sector and the specialist child guidance clinics in CAMHS which were based on a psychoanalytical model of working (Kurtz et al., 1994). A four-tier structure was designed to streamline the referral process for children who could be helped with minor emotional and behavioural problems at Tier 1 by GPs, teachers, practitioners and health visitors. This progressed through the tiers to Tier 4 where very disturbed young people who were at risk of harming themselves or others could be supported by staff with highly specialist skills in forensic work or eating disorders for example (HAS, 1995). Figure 7.1 illustrates this pyramidal CAMHS structure.

The government under its specific mental health grant *Innovations Fund* tried to stimulate changes in the configuration and delivery of CAMHS services to manage the increasing demand for help from parents and professionals (DoH, 1997a; Arcelus et al., 1999; Walker, 2001a; ONS, 2001, 2002). The main aim was to bridge the gap between primary and specialist care in child and adolescent mental health. This could be achieved through the creation of interprofessional teams working together across old organisational boundaries with one operational manager, or by creating specialist teams of family therapists offering brief therapeutic input for example. In theory the existing child and adolescent mental health service should already have facilitated inter-professional working, but in practice every part of the four-tier structure from primary care through to regional specialist units was overstretched.

One of the vexed questions about effectiveness in the organisation of inter-professional care is the structural inhibitors thwarting attempts to cut across professional boundaries. These can be exemplified by the variety of geographical boundaries covered by health, social services and education authorities (Young and Haynes, 1993; Leathard, 1994). New changes in the NHS structure mean that, with a specific geographical catchment area based on the Primary Care Trust boundaries, services can now be more fluently organised. It is important in this new context to be able to distinguish the type of inter-professional team so that:

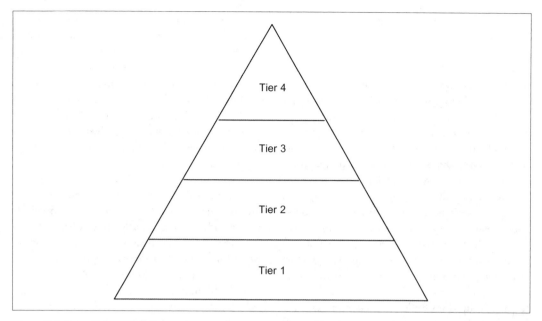

Figure 7.1: Pyramidal CAMHS Structure

■ Practitioners understand their role.

■ Managers can make changes to improve service quality.

■ Planners can decide which type is most suited to the needs of a client population.

■ Researchers can contribute to knowledge about which type is most effective.

(Ovretveit, 1996; Dogra et al., 2002)

One of the issues to emerge from developing new interprofessional CAMHS services is whether at some stage the separate individual professions within each team will begin to lose their former identity and metamorphose into a new kind of practitioner taking on characteristics of their colleagues from different professional backgrounds. There are contemporary examples of such hybrid posts being created in the primary mental health care field, where employers typically advertise for people from any relevant professional background, with appropriate training and experience (Walker, 2003). Having a generic conceptual and practice model such as family therapy could ensure that such teams work from a common theoretical base. A systems perspective could also be a valuable management tool in helping facilitate the examination of

different professional beliefs and the natural rivalries and tensions that follow.

In child and adolescent mental health, the Education, Health and Social Work structural hierarchies have militated against collaboration, preserved separate role identities, and inhibited inter-professional working (Fagin, 1992; Rawson, 1994; Dimigen et al., 1999). This has thwarted repeated attempts to achieve the much-vaunted seamless service for children and families in difficulties, as recommended as far back as the Children Act (DoH, 1989). The new joint commissioning environment in health and social care enshrined in the Health Act enables new services to be created specifically, and this has generally enabled creative, innovative thinking to flourish within and between agencies (DoH, 1999; Kurtz, 2001).

There is evidence of attempts to foster inter-professional training among primary care staff who come into contact with children and adolescents with mental health problems (Firth et al., 1999; Mun et al., 2001; Sebuliba and Vostanis, 2001). Staff such as health visitors, school nurses, social services support staff, family centre volunteers, general practitioners, education staff, and community paediatricians, usually have separate training on mental health issues without much co-ordination. Offering a family therapy training which is not the preserve of any particular profession can help break down the barriers between staff from different agencies.

Inter-professional training can reflect the aspiration that people who work together should also train together to enable a consistency of approach to the identified difficulty (DfEE, 1998). Internationally, there have been studies designed to identify the inter-professional training needs of staff to enable them to function in integrated service delivery systems for children and young people (Magrab et al., 1997). The conclusions are that policy frameworks focussed on children's service planning missed the opportunity to recognise inter-professional training as a priority and to provide incentives to Universities and other training institutions to develop inter-professional training programmes (DoH/DfEE, 1996). Staff who train and work together from different agencies are more likely to feel less inhibited about offering much welcome consultation, advice, training and support to other staff. This can help bridge some of the gaps left by policy limitations and resource shortages unable to deliver the desired inter-professional environment.

If new family therapy services ensure the availability of time which permits a reflective, considered atmosphere this can optimise professional judgment. This contrasts with previous work experiences that can be characterised by reactive, unplanned, and overburdened workloads permitting little time for considered judgments. This welcome capacity to reflect however, presents possible dilemmas in cases where for example, some staff feel they may not in the short term be addressing the underlying causes of some children's problems, particularly where longer-term input would be valuable. Staff are under pressure to reduce waiting lists and respond quickly to emerging mental health problems with early intervention of a short-term nature (Little and Mount, 1999).

The concern is that this may result in either early re-referral or may indeed result in an eventual need for help from specialist services if short-term input is inadequate or the situation deteriorates. A systems consultation and training

role offering support and advice to other professionals can also contribute to more inter-professional understanding, particularly in the social work, health and education sectors where old contacts and relationships could be employed to positive effect (Walker, 2003a). Establishing new teams in an existing professional network of statutory and voluntary providers within established agencies and a dynamic context of changing resources and multiple initiatives is not easy.

There are opportunities for collaboration between these providers and new teams but there are also challenges in fitting in without duplicating or undermining existing good work. Changes in the network in areas such as school health provision, the *Quality Protects* programme in social services, together with Health Action Zones, Youth Offending Teams, Sure Start, On Track, Education Action Zones, Connexions, and fluctuations in the voluntary sector, emphasise the importance of collaborative meetings to enhance opportunities for maintaining and improving working together principles and integrated provision rather than causing confusion.

There is some potential for confusion about specific services however, because of the variety of voluntary and statutory agencies working in the broad area of family support especially in disadvantaged locations (Hetherington and Baistow, 2001). Church, voluntary, and charitable groups have existed in these locations for many years and created their own distinctive role within the diverse range of formal and informal provision of welfare services. There is in these circumstances the prospect of duplication of effort or at worse, mixed messages to families from different agencies. The inter-professional nature of new teams carries the potential for enabling a better understanding of how the overall picture of support services fits together.

It is possible that, as new teams continue to train together, and develop generic working, there may be some resistance to relinquishing former roles, and even strengthening of the boundaries between professions. The challenge for service managers will be to preserve the distinctive individual professional expertise base but not at the expense of service coherence. When attempting to engage children and families already suffering under the pressure of racism and discrimination it is important that children, families and carers have the maximum choice when engaging with services aiming to meet their needs (Bhui and Olajide, 1999). In addition new teams would benefit from formal service user involvement, especially children and young people separately from parents or carers, at the clinical audit, monitoring, review, and strategic planning levels of the service (Alderson, 2000; Barnes and Warren, 1999; Treseder, 1997). Conventional uni-professional services have tended to miss this opportunity for empowering service users.

CHAPTER 8

Ethical Dilemmas in Working with Families

Introduction

There are several sources of guidance for you in trying to juggle the variety of competing demands on your time and on the ethical dilemmas that contemporary practice present you with. Trying to do this while seeking to integrate and synthesise all the different elements of practice is challenging. Clients, your agency management and professional principles all clamour for attention in your assessment and planning practice. There are professional codes in which the expectations for professional practice are described and defined. There are your duties as prescribed in your job contract and based in part on legislation and practice guidance. And there are the rights of service users that are being defined in the context of government health and social care policies informed by statutes such as the Human Rights Act 1998.

In all of these sources the ethics and values of practice are being indirectly put under the microscope and require careful examination if you are to achieve good practice standards and competencies. The ethics and values inherent in caring practice will help you navigate the sometimes turbulent waters where clients, your employer, the professional code and your personal position are all in conflict. Your duties as an employee and your obligations to service users will sometimes come into conflict causing angst and mixed feelings. It is important that you arrive at a position in which you can feel relatively at ease with your stance on a certain issue or with your practice decisions.

> *Family therapy is at best time-bound. Each generation of family therapists will engage in activities in terms of their own time, place and context. Every generation of psychotherapists will be faced with certain abstract questions of morality, fairness and justice that will only find answers within the actual practice of therapy.*
>
> (Rivett and Street, 2003).

Practitioners have always paid careful attention to the ethical dilemmas in their practice. The power invested by the law in some of your tasks make this imperative. The complexities of the rights of each individual within the family are keenly debated in current practice. In legal situations who is the client? Does each family member have appropriate representation and so on? While the issues can be clarified it is not always simple to solve an ethical dilemma since the rights and interests of the individuals may be in opposition.

Ethical guidelines for family therapists caution the therapist to: 'respect and guard confidences of each individual client' (AAMFT, 1991). This general guideline does not recognise the potentially conflicting individual rights within a family system. Newfield et al. (2000) report that while studies have since recognised the potential conflicts, they fall short of providing therapists with the guidelines needed to apply ethical decision making in practice. Let us think about the 'B' family from Chapter 2:

'B' Family

Mother, father and their two children, boys aged eight and five, live together with their maternal grandmother. The parents are having difficulty with the elder boy's behaviour and the referral suggests that they are being undermined by interference from Grandma.

In Chapter 2 we were considering who to invite to the first interview bearing in mind the possibility that the parenting subsystem may be being undermined by the grandmother's interference. Here we need to think about issues such as why the grandmother is living with the family. What are her care needs? We may become aware during our contact with the family that she has some features which could be characteristic of a dementing illness which the family do not seem aware of. At what point, if at all, should this kind of individual information be shared with the family? What impact may it be having on the reasons that the family presented for therapy? The ethical guideline to 'respect and guard confidences of each individual client' suddenly begins to seem extremely complex and we find ourselves faced with an ethical dilemma.

What is an ethical dilemma in family therapy practice?

One possible definition is proposed by Burkemper, 'Family therapists make ethical decisions. An ethical dilemma presents the therapist with two or more good reasons to make two or more reasonable decisions' (Burkemper, 2002). This captures the core of the dilemma, that is: that there is more than one reasonable decision which could be made and therefore, there has to be some ethical basis on which to make a decision. Even within this notion there are many ways of understanding what would or would not be an ethical decision.

We will begin by looking at the different types of reasoning that can be used to underpin decisions in practice. Firstly, the concepts of **care reasoning** and **justice reasoning** can be used to approach a dilemma in its simplest form. Further concepts, including **duty-to-warn** and **rights to autonomy** will then be explored as all these aspects need to be considered as part of any ethical decision making process.

What is the evidence base for ethical decision making? The development of ethical practice is an ongoing task. In this chapter, the subject is approached by examining some of the recent research into ethical decision making. This will serve to define the components of ethical decision making and give a base from which to consider the dilemmas faced in practice by family therapists. The papers described give some answers to the question of what the evidence is and also give an opportunity to consider some specific issues such as participation in research and ethical responsibilities of parents with chronic illnesses such as diabetes.

Care reasoning and justice reasoning

What are care and justice reasoning? Essentially, the two types of reasoning propose a value base which can underpin ethical decisions. The care perspective considers the actual consequences of a decision for the involved parties: how the decision would affect the relationship, the context, the need to avoid hurt, and the issues of altruism. Justice reasoning highlights issues of fairness, rights and obligation. Clearly a decision based on justice reasoning may also take care reasoning into account. The point of separating these two concepts is to try to understand which type of reasoning is dominant in different situations and whether therapists agree about this. Evidence from a number of studies suggests that real life and hypothetical dilemmas elicit different responses, and it has been suggested that the impersonal nature of the hypothetical dilemma might elicit a justice response. If this were the case then research, using hypothetical examples, would tend to overestimate the use of justice reasoning by therapists.

Newfield et al., (2000) in a paper entitled: *Ethical Decision Making among Family Therapists and Individual Therapists* explored the use of these two types of reasoning as the bases for ethical decision making. In this study informants responded to three ethical dilemmas, two hypothetical and one real; and all the interviews were assessed for **Care Reasoning** and **Justice Reasoning**.

The reason that the researchers decided to look at this particular dichotomy was that family therapy has been criticised for lacking ethics. The particular focus of this criticism is the apparent lack of consideration for the rights of the individual in a theoretical paradigm that focuses on systems, where existing ethical models used by mental health professional organisations focus on individual rights. To test the impact of the therapists theoretical perspective on decision making a structured interview was used with both family and individual therapists. You would expect that the family therapists and the individual therapists would reach different decisions since the individual therapists would focus on the concerns of an individual client, and the family therapists would be dealing with the dilemma of the individual clients' concerns and the impact on the family system.

The three dilemmas are described below. As you read these, try to pause and think about the decisions you would make as a practitioner or family therapist working with the family. Dilemma 1 is particularly important to self appraise and we suggest putting the book down and having a coffee break, to really identify a situation from your own practice which you will then be able to monitor in relation to all the issues raised in this chapter.

Dilemma 1: Real-life

I am trying to understand how therapists make difficult choices in their professional practice. I would like you to tell me about a difficult choice you have had to make, a decision that involved a situation where you weren't sure what to do.

Dilemma 2: Individual-hypothetical

After many sessions a client informs you that he has tested positive for AIDS. When you discuss this with him, he demonstrates an understanding of the disease process and mode of transition. Although the client has been aware of this condition for several months he has continued to engage in sexual relationships,

and also indicates an unwillingness to discontinue sexual activity or to discuss this information with past and present sexual partners.

Dilemma 3: Family-hypothetical

A family referred itself to your office to address communication issues. The family consisted of five persons at home: Mother, Father, two daughters and a son. After several sessions, it was disclosed that father had sexually abused the oldest daughter. The father had stopped the abuse several months ago, and the family indicated that the primary reason for seeking therapy was to address issues related to the abuse. The family members had kept this a secret and only confided in you with the request that you not appraise or involve others because they felt the problem was being resolved. To date, this family has worked hard in therapy, and all family members, including the father and daughter, seem highly motivated to continue the therapy. The father has agreed to a contract with you regarding the issues of abuse.

In the research, family therapists (n = 30) and individual therapists (n = 30) were each interviewed in relation to these three dilemmas to see whether they used the care or justice reasoning and whether there were any differences between the groups of therapists. Before continuing, consider whether you have based your decision on either predominantly care or predominantly justice reasoning.

What were the results of the study?

Firstly, there was no significant difference between individual and family therapists in relation to each of the dilemmas. There was also no significant interaction between gender and dilemma type. That is, the decisions made were not influenced by the therapist being either individual or family orientated. Faced with any of these dilemmas family therapists and individual therapists were just as likely to use either care or justice reasoning.

Secondly, there was a significant difference within the dilemmas. That is, there was a significant difference across the care scores for each dilemma regardless of therapist type or gender. The therapists were making care based decisions more than 50 per cent of the time on all dilemmas, with the personal dilemma eliciting the highest number of care based decisions.

In this study striking similarities emerged between individual and family therapists in ethical decision making suggesting that factors other than theoretical orientation were influencing their decisions. Both had adopted a model of decision making that focussed on values identified with an ethic of care. There was significantly more care reasoning demonstrated on the personal dilemma than on the hypothetical dilemmas. 'When the outcome of this study is viewed with an understanding that the ethical codes of professional organisations emphasise a justice ethic, it clarifies the concerns professionals express about professional ethical codes.' (Newfield et al., 2000).

The findings of this study are really quite astonishing. Firstly, that despite individual or systems orientations therapists are likely to respond to ethical dilemmas in the same way. Secondly, the therapist's responses to ethical dilemmas are based on care reasoning in over half the decisions. Given that the codes of ethics for all therapists emphasise justice reasoning this is an important finding.

What happened to justice reasoning? The rhetoric amongst professionals would indicate that the legal frameworks within which they work determine what they are able to do. Yet the reality of working with families brings the care reasoning to the fore presumably at times, in situations which could place one or more family members at risk. This is why the codes of ethics for professionals emphasise justice reasoning – to protect – but there is clearly a discrepancy between rhetoric and reality. Bearing these findings in mind it will now be useful to look at research focussing on duty-to-warn situations.

Duty-to-Warn Situations

Burkemper (2002) in a paper titled: *Family Therapists' Ethical Decision-Making Processes in Two Duty-To-Warn Situations* used two scenarios to try and understand the processes involved in ethical decision-making by marital and family therapists. The dilemma investigated was that of protecting client confidentiality when there was a perceived or actual duty-to-warn. The decision to protect client confidentiality or to reveal information to authorities or to other family members was examined in response to two scenarios of child abuse and of HIV transmission to unsuspecting partners.

Dilemma 1: Child abuse
In a therapy session your client informs you that they have been disciplining their child with the buckle end of the belt that leaves welts on the child. The client will not contract to end their use of this form of discipline. The client will not authorise you to share this information with anyone.

Dilemma 2: HIV
In a therapy session, your client informs you that they are HIV positive and are engaging in unprotected sex with their uninformed mate. The client will not authorise you to share this information with anyone.

The basis of ethical decision making includes lower and higher-level components. The lower-level decision components include personal/therapeutic response, professional ethics, and legal considerations or laws of the State. The higher-level decision components include non-maleficence (avoiding harm), autonomy (individuals' right to decision making), beneficence (doing well), fidelity (client's right to confidentiality), and justice (being fair to my client). Respondents (n = 177) were asked to rank order these components to indicate which were most and which least important in their decision making in relation to these two dilemmas. All respondents were members of the American Association of Marital and Family Therapists (AAMFT).

Statistical results indicated that in the child abuse scenario, professional ethics and legal considerations or laws of the State were considered most important. In the HIV scenario, professional ethics were considered most important. Across both scenarios, the preferred higher-level

Table 8.1: Order of importance of the principles in relation to scenarios of child abuse and HIV

Child abuse	HIV
Avoiding harm	Avoiding harm
Doing good – beneficience	Confidentiality
Being fair – justice	Being fair – justice
Confidentiality	Autonomy
Autonomy	Doing good – beneficience

decision base was nonmaleficent, that is, avoiding harm. There were differences between the child abuse and HIV scenarios in the perceived significance of the remaining higher-level decision base items, see Table 8.1.

The idea of this research was to identify the potential hierarchy of preferences in ethical decision making. 'Ethical decision making is often viewed as an abstract enterprise. This research should, however, provoke a sense of identifying and putting into words the possible components in ethical decision making.' (Burkemper, 2002). The author hoped that the idea of breaking ethical decision making into discrete elements could be used in teaching, supervision and self-analysis of practice decisions. This certainly seems a valuable enterprise since at times lives may rest upon our ability to deal with ethical dilemmas appropriately. These concepts can be used in all situations where there could be competing claims from individuals within a family system.

Unlike the previous study legal considerations and laws of the state were considered most important. This is somewhat reassuring after the results of the previous study given that laws and legal requirements are there for good reason. However, this finding may be dependent on the clarity of the scenarios and we know that in real life even situations of child abuse are often not clear and that there will be scope for interpretation of the timing and appropriateness of legal interventions. We would suggest that this is where the scope for care reasoning to override justice reasoning lies.

Having grasped these core concepts in relation to competing claims of individuals it will be interesting to consider a situation where the basis of the ethical dilemma is between which concepts

to place greatest value on in relation to one family member's well-being.

Ethical dilemmas with elderly people – beneficence versus autonomy

The issues of beneficence (doing good) versus autonomy (individual's right to decision making) may arise in a number of care situations. These issues are clearly identified and researched in an article on family care of older persons. There is a tendency to think of family therapy as mainly relating to families with children, but family therapy in modern practice is highly relevant to families at all stages of the life cycle.

Families have always been and continue to be the main caregivers for frail and elderly relatives. Barber and Lyness (2001) in their article: *Ethical Issues in Family Care of Older People with Dementia: Implications for Family Therapists* highlight some of the ethical dilemmas families face in caring for an elderly loved one, particularly focussing on those caring for elderly parents suffering from a dementing illness.

Families face a number of ethical dilemmas relating to the dependent care of an elderly relative including:

- Determining the extent of filial responsibility.
- Family equity.
- Competing commitments.
- Care recipient's autonomy and safety/decision making.
- Knowing what the care recipient wants.
- Financing the cost of care.

What the care receiver wants may not always be in her or his best interests, at least from the perspective of the caregiver. Dilemma 1 is an example of this.

Dilemma 1: Who decides?

A person wants to continue to drive even though their mental capacity makes this activity dangerous to both themselves and others.

This is difficult for the caregiver who has to weigh up whether to let the care receiver continue to drive (respecting their autonomy) or whether to take away the keys viewing their and others safety as more important. 'Often family members let beneficence overrule the principle of autonomy while feeling guilty about taking away some of the elderly person's independence.' Barber and Lyness (2001) see an important role for systemic therapists in working with families facing these dilemmas by helping the family to deal with its internal needs and the decisions relating to the wider system including health care providers.

When ethical principles are in conflict as in the example above Barber and Lyness suggest using the principles of **universalisability** and **balancing**. 'When utilising the criterion of universalisability, therapists ask themselves: "Would I want this decision applied to me, my family or all other families in similar situations?" According to the criterion of balancing, "An ethical decision is one that produces the least amount of avoidable harm to all individuals involved".' (Barber and Lyness, 2001). This sounds simple and sensible but we know from the examples of the earlier studies that it is not simple, nor is it easy to decide when is exactly the right time to curtail a person's autonomy. It is easy to intervene too soon or too late! The next dilemma is particularly acute in relation to the timing of interventions.

Dilemma 2: Own home or residential care?

Whether to sacrifice the care recipient's autonomy in favour of restrictions (e.g. institutional care) which are in the recipient's best interests but may be prejudicial to the care recipient's well-being as well (i.e. how will they react to the change).

In this situation it is difficult to balance the needs of the care receiver (for autonomy) and the needs of the caregiver (to support the care receiver's safety). What is more important? Their safety or autonomy and who should make this decision? If the safety of third parties is involved it is easier to take the decision to limit an individual's autonomy. If it is only their own safety which is at risk the ethical dilemmas are experienced most acutely. There is a clear role for working with the family here. All too often decisions are made by family members on behalf of each other without a family meeting to explore the issues together. Generally it is the professionals who fear what will happen if the family are brought together but the reality is that this offers a chance to share together in what are extremely painful decisions at this stage of the life cycle.

A further ethical principle which can come into play in decisions relating to elderly family members is **justice**. That is the notion of fairly distributing care giving responsibilities among family members and of the need to preserve the well-being of the caregiver. Hasselkus (1991) interviewed 60 caregivers and found that most placed the needs of the care recipient above their own, although this did not occur without feelings of resentment and guilt. For family therapists and practitioners it is important to explore the family's view of justice as these views reveal the caregivers implicit ethical code and will help the family with their decisions.

There is no clear ethical code to guide the ethical decisions of caregivers and their families. Therapists must be able to work with the individual differences between families. For example, families may differ in the value they place on the person with advanced dementia. Faced with a family member's disintegration they may need help in deciding what the goals of their care should be. The family therapist or practitioner can help keep a focus on the family system: as with a range of professionals dealing with a patient with dementia many medical clinicians, of necessity, become problem oriented. Family therapists may be in a unique position to help families make ethically sound decisions as they struggle with caregiving since they are able to access the ethical issues for the family system rather than focussing on the needs of one member.

There can be other dilemmas in relation to health for the family, and the section below raises such issues which are pertinent to all those working with families.

Ethical dilemmas in health care

The physical health of family members is another arena where there can be competing claims. Parents have a role in deciding medical treatments for their children, where the inexact state of knowledge about best treatments in most conditions can cause difficulties. One potential scenario, choice of treatment for a child with depression will be considered in the next section.

With some ongoing conditions there can be conflict caused by the condition, for example, the control of diabetes in pregnancy. The health of the mother during pregnancy directly impacts on the outcome for the baby.

> There has been a change from a hierarchical model of delivering care, in which health professionals take on full responsibility, to one in which responsibility is shared and there is a partnership between the person with diabetes and the health care professional . . . Whether these models are applicable to pregnancy has received little attention.
>
> (Josse et al., 2003).

If the diabetes is poorly controlled who should take responsibility?

In health care the Common Law principles relating to **capacity**, **best interest** and **duty of care** form the ethical bases for decision making. Central to these principles is the idea that every adult has the right to decide whether or not to accept or refuse medical treatment. The reasons for refusal are irrelevant as long as the person has the capacity to make the decision.

The practitioner and other professionals working with such dilemmas will not find any easy answers. Family support at the present time is particularly interested in models of partnership and empowerment and the situation of diabetes control in pregnancy, throws into sharp relief the

ethical dilemmas which can be raised when working in partnership. This would be particularly acute when the partnership is of a pseudo nature as the practitioner has legal responsibilities in some situations which would take precedence. The ideas from evidence based practice can give some help in treatment and intervention decisions but they are far from perfect and need viewing with caution, as is suggested by Ryan (2002).

Ethical safeguards for research subjects

Research is meant to provide a balanced and unbiased view of the topic researched. Is this possible? What factors might influence both who participates in research and the content of its inquiry? In order to undertake research, funding is needed. If the funders have a vested interest in the outcome then the research or dissemination of findings could be influenced by this. The paper by Ryan (2002): *Safeguards for Research Subjects: Who's Watching Whom?* identifies some of the ethical dilemmas in the research process when working with vulnerable populations.

This clinical report, from an adult mental health perspective, identifies the need for a public forum for discussion and debate when research subjects are recruited from vulnerable populations and/or groups with impaired ability to make decisions. 'In all of these debates, mental health advocacy groups represent a valued and valuable player. Are their concerns regarding research in the mental health field warranted? Yes. Should research using psychiatrically ill patients therefore be banned? No.' (Ryan, 2002).

The paper goes on to consider the dilemmas and competing needs of the researchers, the patients and their advocates. Ryan says that most researchers recognise the need for feedback from mental health advocacy groups, even if they do not welcome it. On the other hand there are times when mental health groups act other than concerned advocates of ill patients. At other times a paternalistic attitude creeps in under the presumption that a person with a psychiatric illness cannot make an informed decision. This paternalism can originate from an overly concerned family member, an advocacy group, or the clinician, and may not represent a patient's wish to participate in a research study or clinical trial.

The ethical issues raised in this paper are important to discuss in both therapy and research and are relevant to all vulnerable populations. This point is highlighted also by a study considering childhood depression. 'There is no definitive course of treatment for children with depression. Each treatment option, therefore, has ethical implications for both providers and families. Providers must balance the principles of beneficence and nonmaleficience for the patient. Parents must be allowed autonomy in selecting the best treatment course for their child.' (Nelson, 2003).

One approach to this decision making would be to base the decision on evidence-based research. However, as we have seen, research also has ethical concerns (Ryan, 2002; Kerridge et al., 1998). Further treatment studies are needed in childhood depression. This involves both the parents giving consent and the children giving assent. Ethical assent with children needs to be appropriate to their developmental stage and preferably proposed by a neutral practitioner to help minimise pressure to participate, whilst at the same time recognising the potential importance for treatment advances.

One of the problems with evidence-based practice is that inevitably, as we can see from the studies above, evidence is limited. Over time the 'best' way to treat any condition changes, and in many instances in both medical and social care there are no guarantees for the outcome of an intervention. Thus we can use, but not rely on, guidelines and ethical appraisal, in itself determined by time and place: and context, is critical (Rivett and Street, 2003).

A number of studies have focussed on ethical considerations in family therapy practice including ethical concerns for families participating in research. These issues are crucial to respecting the rights of the individual family members whilst working with the family system. It is very helpful for therapists to keep these ideas as key to their negotiations and interventions with families since there is constant possibility for competing claims amongst family members. What is best for one family member may not be best for other members. Here, in a way, is the great value of working with the whole family system since these dilemmas have to be resolved and may be part of the reason that the family has come to therapy. When just one family member is worked with these crucial ethical dilemmas may not even be identified and cannot be resolved without the cooperation and working together of the whole family.

These ethical dilemmas can arise at any stage in the life cycle, though are particularly easy to identify when working with families with concerns about the welfare and care of elderly members or with children and young people. We are also influenced by ideas and procedures current at the time (Rivett and Street, 2003). Ethically sound decisions will, in effect, be time and context bound. For the professional working with the family the balance of care and justice reasoning should be held as important principles along with legal frameworks. The question of duty to warn and of the components of ethical practice, including confidentiality, beneficence and autonomy should be visited with each family to ensure ethical and anti-oppressive practice.

CHAPTER 9

Evaluation and Effectiveness

Introduction

Family therapy is used in a variety of contexts, as we have noted earlier, and is perhaps more commonly associated with child and family problems where concerns have been expressed about the behaviour of an individual child. In child care work it can also feature where a context of abuse, neglect, parental mental ill health, or domestic violence requires an assessment of the impact on the child or young person as well as efforts to promote a more protective environment. These can be addressed in a mixture of specialist resources, primary care interventions, or in statutory and voluntary contexts where family therapy approaches and systems theory are used as an aid to decision-making and the preparation of official reports. Practitioners have the basic skills required to adopt a family therapy approach in work that can prevent problems deteriorating, or in assessment for further intervention by other agencies, or substitute resources such as fostering or residential care.

As caring work adjusts to an organisational climate where cost-effectiveness, audit and evaluation are expected to contribute to the growing evidence base of practice, staff need to know what works in order to justify their intervention. One of the major problems in attempting to ascertain what works is in distinguishing the impact your particular intervention has had in the context of the multiple influences on a family's existence. They could be receiving a number of interventions from several agencies such as school, health visiting, social work, youth offending, each of which or a combination of all could be having a significant effect. It is also the case that any or all could be contributing to a deterioration in the situation. Some argue that family support is not appropriate to evidence-based approaches to practice because unlike medicine and experimental research, family support is in a dynamic, interconnected relationship with clients the nature of which cannot be subjected to conventional research methodology, examining inputs and outcomes (Webb, 2001).

Research into family therapy can be considered compatible with the process and practice of the model itself. As the modern physical scientists have evolved new ways of thinking about facts and objectivity, so with systems theory the social sciences can embrace the concepts of progressive hypothesising – formulating ideas about a family, testing them and then reformulating on the basis of feedback (Dallos and Draper, 2000). As we noted earlier, the use of supervision, videotape recording and family tasks offer a rich source of evidence with which to measure and analyse the impact of the therapy. Systems theory also sits comfortably within new paradigms in the health and social sciences which seek to look beyond observed behaviours and recognise the importance of the meanings and beliefs created by families about their problems and attempted solutions.

Types of evaluation

It is a useful start to think about evaluation by distinguishing between subjective and objective approaches. **Subjective evaluation** concentrates on gauging how clients have experienced what you and your agency have offered them. **Objective evaluation** involves identifying particular objectives in the work and then deciding whether or not these have been achieved (Walker and Beckett, 2004). Subjective evaluation could be carried out either through discussion or through some form of questionnaire, either in the company of a practitioner or not. Or you might also wish to think about how, in devising a questionnaire, you could focus on partnership and empowerment by:

▓ Asking specific questions on degree of involvement, for example whether the client felt they were properly listened to.
▓ Working together with the service user to make sure the questionnaire reflected their agenda.
▓ Looking at whether the outcome of intervention was satisfactory, and if not how it could be done differently.
▓ Tackling issues of power and discrimination such as asking particular questions related to the service users needs as a woman, a black person, lesbian or gay, or someone with a disability.

With objective evaluation your objectives will depend on your particular work setting. The important point is that they are clearly measurable such as:

▓ Removal from the child protection register, or return home.
▓ A young person finding accommodation or a job.
▓ Finding an adoptive family.
▓ Maintaining an older person in their own home.
▓ Improving a child's school attendance.
▓ Helping a person avoid readmission to psychiatric hospital.

Central to the ideas of efficiency and effectiveness within evaluation is the concept of **quality assurance**. Judgments as to whether services are up to the standard expected have traditionally been based on whether the right amount of care

was being provided rather than the quality of care. The question 'Are we doing things right?' has been supplemented by the question 'Are we doing the right things?' Below are some of the approaches to determining the quality of care.

Inspection

Since the NHS and Community Care Act 1990 **inspection units** were created within social service departments separate from the day-to-day management function of monitoring residential provision. Currently a new system of inspection is being inaugurated which completely separates inspection from those providing residential care. Apart from the physical environment in these homes inspectors should elicit the views of residents and staff. The limitations of this approach are:

▓ In depth understanding is constrained due to the volume of work to be carried out and the limited contact with everyone concerned.
▓ It is difficult to be objective when you are working for the same authority responsible for running the home.
▓ Inspectors will invariably come with their own perceptions and values and may not be able to involve service users or staff as fully as they should.

Reviews

The idea of a **review** is that an organisation should prepare its plans on a regular basis and that progress towards the **achievement of objectives and targets** set out in those plans should be subjected to scrutiny. These plans are submitted to central government in accordance with guidelines laid down as part of overall strategic planning. This macro level has its parallel with the micro level of your work with clients. The limitations of reviews are:

▓ Organisational reviews relate to whether the plan is being conformed to usually in terms of budget and efficiency. These issues can take precedence over questions of appropriateness and acceptability.

- Service user representatives may be consulted during the process of devising plans but they are primarily the domain of senior management staff.
- The views and expectations of field staff, carers and clients, are not paramount despite rhetoric in mission statements avowing to empower users.

Performance assessment

Central government has begun to issue guidance in the form of national comparative data from many local authorities and health and social care organisations to judge particular **aspects of performance**. The white paper *Modernising Social Services* (DoH, 1998d) for example set out new arrangements to assess the performance of each council within the wider Best Value regime that requires local authorities to achieve improved cost effectiveness. These have been translated into targets for services to attain, for example the number of children on the child protection registers, or the number of home care organisers per head of population. Local authorities are awarded star ratings on a range of performance measures. This framework is designed to improve services that people receive by:

- Helping councils develop their own performance management arrangements.
- Ensuring that corporate management and political scrutiny promotes better social services that contribute to community well-being.
- Ensuring that councils work effectively with the NHS to address joint health and social care policy and service delivery issues.
- Assessing councils' progress in implementing government policies for social care.
- Identifying and promoting best practice.
- Identifying councils that are performing poorly and ensuring they take action to improve.

They are criticised as crude measures that do not adequately reflect the individual characteristics of different parts of the country, and the levels of need within them. Little account seems to be taken of the differences and distinctions between inner city deprived neighbourhoods, leafy suburbs, or remote rural communities. These misleading measures do not adequately reflect subtle changes and improvements that might disproportionately impact on the quality of service users' lives but do not show up in broad statistical data. The issue of resources is notably absent from the above list. Their limitations are:

- Although they aim to improve standards of care the preparation of performance indicators does not involve the intended beneficiaries.
- Their quantitative nature stresses procedures and outcomes rather than effectiveness and acceptability.
- Their compilation presupposes that local authorities have uniform, accurate, and comprehensive comparable information systems.
- They take little account of variations in the priority given by different authorities to aspects of their care services.

Some of the key indicators used to measure performance include:

- Information on education, employment and training for care leavers.
- Placement stability for looked after children in the short term and longer term.
- The percentage of children looked after in foster placements or placed for adoption.
- The percentage of children on the child protection registers.

Satisfaction surveys

The collection of qualitative, highly personal data offers another perspective on the issue of service planning and evaluation of provision. Asking clients what they think of current services seems straightforward, and there are procedures publicised that offer the public an avenue to pursue grievances or register compliments. However **satisfaction surveys** cannot counterbalance the organisations' attempts to determine performance. The danger is that the act of conducting a survey can be seen as an end in itself. Unless such surveys are backed up with action plans and a set of measurable improvements based on them they can end up being viewed as at best tokenistic and at worse deeply patronising. Further limitations are:

■ They often assume that the person asked has knowledge of alternative provision.
■ Satisfaction may not tell much about the quality of the service since the client may be starting from a low expectation.
■ Data derived from questionnaires is limited when alternatives such as case studies, personal diaries or group interviews could yield richer information.

How to evaluate

Many practitioners tend to avoid evaluation or to interpret it in such a way that it comes to mean a brief retrospective review of a piece of work or an initiative. Such work can be undertaken by academic researchers with no real stake in the quality of service provision or understanding of the subtle complexities of therapeutic work. You may also hold the view that your agency has to collect so much performance-related information for the government that anything that appears to detract from work with service users and your primary responsibilities has to be avoided. However, accountable practice demands that public services need to justify what they do and find useful ways of demonstrating this.

An **action evaluation model** has been developed in Bradford (Fawcett, 2000) which is based on a partnership between the University, Social Services Dept, and the Health Trust, and which is aimed at demystifying the evaluation process and providing staff with the tools and support to conduct evaluations. Action evaluations take place in the workplace, and focus on areas viewed as important by those involved – with the findings feeding into the services being studied. Such a model can be adapted to evaluate your individual work or a service based on a family therapy approach. These are the main characteristics:

■ **Outline the current situation** – collect baseline information and establish the service's overall aims and objectives. This can include quantitative data such as the numbers using a service, and qualitative data such as details of service users' experiences.
■ **Specify available resources, overall aim and objectives** – any project or initiative is likely to have a number of objectives but it is important to be specific about them and what the broad overall purpose of the activity is.
■ **Link goals to specific objectives** – identifying the desired outcomes or goals enable you to work backwards through any intermediary stages in the process. This helps to provide progress indicators and how goals can be achieved.
■ **Detail why the agreed objectives and goals were decided upon** – no evaluation goes strictly according to plan therefore it is important to record how goals were established. A record needs to be kept of the reasoning behind the aims, and any deviation clearly stated and made transparent. This information needs to be easily retrievable so it can be used to explain why goals have changed.
■ **Monitor and review the activity** –information from all stakeholders can be collated including recommendations for changing or improving the service. Activity related to goals can be appraised, and evidence of progress summarised. It is important to document how and why progress was made and what obstacles were encountered. This data can be fed back to service purchasers and planners reflecting an inclusive, bottom-up approach to evaluation.

Does family therapy work?

There have been increasing numbers of studies of family therapy attempting to measure the effectiveness of this particular therapeutic intervention since it began to be more comprehensively established in the 1970s (Lask, 1979; Campbell and Draper, 1985; Reimers and Treacher, 1995; Dallos and Draper, 2000). On the whole the evidence is consistent that family therapy is a valuable and effective approach to use in a variety of contexts. Before examining some of the studies to gain some detail about how family therapy helped it needs to be acknowledged that most of the studies have been undertaken in 'clinical' settings. There have been relatively few studies of family therapy employed in front line agency contexts. Indeed the valid evidence base for interventions is generally speaking rather thin – but improving. However, even within the confines of clinical practice it is clear that family therapy has established itself alongside some of the older and more orthodox therapeutic methods and models of intervention as a reliable and acceptable approach. A meta-analysis of the findings of 163 published and unpublished outcome studies on the efficacy and effectiveness of marital and family therapy concluded that the clients did significantly better than untreated control group clients (Shadish et al., 1995). Based on recent substantial literature search of the available research some clear findings demonstrate (Friedlander, 2001; Goldenberg and Goldenberg, 2004):

- Compared with no treatment, non-behavioural marital/family therapies are effective in two thirds of all cases.
- The efficacy of systemic, behavioural, emotionally focussed, and insight-producing family therapies is established for marital and adolescent delinquent problems.
- Structural family therapy appears to be particularly helpful for certain childhood and adolescent psychosomatic symptoms.
- There is evidence for the efficacy of family therapy in treating childhood conduct disorders, phobias, anxieties, and especially autism.

The research evidence

A major review of consumer studies of family therapy and marital counselling analysed a variety of research including large and small scale studies, individual case studies, specific therapeutic methodologies and ethnographic studies (Treacher, 1995). These are particularly valuable sources of evidence because whilst they do not have the same methodological rigour as 'clinical'

research studies, they nevertheless reflect a more realistic experience of families in front-line working contexts. The review concluded that practitioners who neglected the service user perspective and undervalued the personal relationship aspects of their family support work in favour of concentrating on inducing change, ran the risk of creating considerable dissatisfaction among service users. This reinforced findings from an earlier study into the effectiveness of family therapy that advised that advice and directive work needs to be balanced with reflective and general supportive elements (Howe, 1989). In particular the following conclusions are worth highlighting:

- Families needed an explanation of what therapy was about and how it differed from regular service contact.
- Families felt they were being investigated, judged, manipulated and maligned and were unable to discuss issues they felt were important.

These studies point up the dilemmas faced by practitioners trying to employ therapeutic techniques in the context of a statutory remit which often includes a coercive element to family participation and an inspectorial or monitoring element to the work. Assessment in social work is for example expected to include a therapeutic element but in the context of determining whether a child is in need or child protection concerns, it is understandable if both parents and practitioners lose track of the purpose of such assessments. These dilemmas probably also reflect artificial time constraints which are inherently anti-therapeutic. As with similar studies in other health and social care organisations it is difficult to draw substantive extrapolations from the data examining family therapy in practice because they rarely meet research validity and reliability criteria. Thus, attempts to compare findings usually run into methodological problems that negate any meaningful meta-analysis.

In a sense these findings confirm our view that attempting to use family therapy approaches needs to be thought through, planned, and introduced in a way that best fits with the context of service users. Families who have had regular contact with agencies regarding child care issues will have learned a number of responses to their patterns of contact with, and relationships towards, staff. Parents could have a perception of practitioners as interfering, undermining nosey parkers which contextualises their behaviour and communications with them. On the other hand they could perceive practitioners as rescuers, troubleshooters, or mediators between them and difficult teenagers.

In either perception a number of roles may be prescribed which affect the emotional dynamics between them and the practitioner. This could range from parents infantilising themselves resulting in behaviour that elicits an authoritative or parental response; through to aggressive or hostile behaviour that elicits a compliant or collusive response from the practitioner. These patterns of interaction need to be thoroughly understood in order to figure out the most appropriate way of using a family therapy approach. Fortunately, as a flexible approach, there is a wide range of options to select from as we noted earlier.

It is also important to take account of the natural history and environmental context of children's problems in relation to their developmental stage and acknowledge that there are no standardised ways of measuring childhood functioning. As discussed earlier many of these classic measures are based on white Eurocentric models that are not nowadays consistent with culturally competent practice. What is consistent in all the major studies is the general absence and rarity of service user evaluation of, and involvement in, the design of child and family research. The implication is that by enlarging the focus of effectiveness measures it is possible to see children not just with problems but also as having positive and constructive elements in their family lives and building on these and amplifying them wherever possible. They also have much to tell us about how *they* feel about research into their lives and how methodologies can become more child-centred.

This view is echoed in recommendations based on thorough research into interventions targeted at the child, teacher and parent that demonstrate that the combined effect produces the most sustained reduction in conflict problems, both at home and at school, and in peer relationships (Webster-Stratton, 1997). Recognising and building on the children's own perspectives provides new opportunities for work with children and families guided by possibilities adults are not aware of or fail to pay enough attention to. Thus it is possible to adhere to the Children Act tenets of the paramountcy of the child's welfare whilst employing a systems theoretical paradigm that permits an effective analysis of the child's emotional, psychological and environmental family context.

Children in families

Children's perspectives have rarely been explored in relation to the help they receive towards their emotional and mental well-being (Hill et al., 1995; Gordon and Grant, 1997). The prevalence and upward trends of mental health problems in childhood together with findings that young people with such difficulties are reluctant to make use of specialist services or quickly cease contact is worrying (Mental Health Foundation, 1999; Audit Commission, 1999; Richardson and Joughin, 2000). This indicates the importance of developing appropriate sources of help that are experienced as useful and relevant and therefore going to be used effectively.

In order to do that, methods of consulting with children and young people need to be developed that are appropriate, effective and methodologically robust. The family therapy literature has tended to neglect the individual experience and the voice of the child is almost unheard in most evaluative studies. Here practitioners have the opportunity of refining the orthodox family therapy model to include a child's eye perspective. The skill is in having the intellectual agility and confidence to move between the therapeutic dimension and the statutory or service level dimension during the same piece of work. Joint work or specialist supervision or consultation can help.

There is a growing literature on the subject of the rights of children and young people to influence decisions about their own health and healthcare (MacFarlane and McPherson, 1995;

Treseder, 1997; Wilson, 1999; Alderson, 2000). However, this remains an area of contention for some professionals who believe that the notion that children can think, comment, and participate in a meaningful way in evaluations of the help they receive, is at best misguided or at worst undermining of parental and professional responsibility. There is perhaps added poignancy when this concept is applied to child and family work, where the very emotional and behavioural problems of children give weight to the argument against seeking children's perceptions.

Parents and those with parental responsibility might present powerful arguments for wanting to make exclusive decisions to enable them to cope with and manage sometimes worrying and disturbing behaviour. Equally, where children's difficulties are located in the context of parental discord, abuse, domestic violence or family dynamics it is important to ensure children are not blamed or scapegoated for problems caused by events or actions outside their control (Cooper, 1999; Sutton, 1999; Dallos and Draper, 2000). Practitioners using family therapy approaches need to be sensitive to the power dynamics operating against children and young people in family systems, especially where they are the identified patient or problem.

Research evidence demonstrates the value of consulting children and seeing how much they can achieve with a little help which is appropriate and acceptable (Levine, 1993; Griffiths, 1998). Children, like adults, have the right, under the terms of the UN Convention, to be consulted with, and to express their views about, services provided for them (UN, 1989 Article 12). In some public services in England there is a legal duty to consult them in order to ascertain their wishes and feelings (Children Act, 1989). An examination of some contemporary contributions on the subject of consulting with children and young people reveals a mixed picture in terms of effectiveness, inclusion, methodologies, and ethical considerations.

A children's rights perspective

Several studies provide some evidence of the effectiveness of attempts to ascertain the percep-

tions of children and young people about services they have received. There is among some practitioners and researchers a general assumption that seeking the views of children and young people is of itself a good thing. Yet the purpose of gaining such perceptions can be varied, the methods employed quite different, and the evidence of the impact of seeking their views, obscure. Given the power differential between parents and children, combined with the way families can scapegoat individual children, it is very important to consider ways of ascertaining their feelings about work being undertaken. Using a family therapy approach should not mean abandoning the experience of the individual participants.

Hennessey (1999) in a meta-review of a collection of research studies on this subject concluded that with the increasing interest in seeking children's views there need to be better developed instruments for measuring satisfaction and gaining children's evaluation of the services they receive. Research on children's evaluations of education, paediatrics, and child mental health services was assessed. Only a minority of studies examined had presented information on the structure, reliability and validity of the instruments they used. Most of the studies concerned education contexts, the paediatric studies treated parents as the sole clients, while in mental health studies the correspondence between children's and parents evaluations of services seemed to be greater.

The majority of studies used some form of questionnaire to collect information from children. Little information about the administration of these questionnaires was provided in the studies, for instance where they were administered or by whom. Factors that might influence their completion include the gender of the adult involved and whether telephone or postal methods were used. Use of Likert scales revealed little consensus on what were appropriate scales for children of different ages. Only a small number used qualitative methods to gather data.

Hennessey suggests interviews and open-ended questions have the potential to provide valuable information on client evaluations that cannot be tapped by rating scales. Most studies presented limited information on the psychometric properties of the instruments used. Where information was presented it was limited to information on the internal consistency of the instrument used. Only a small number of studies presented any information on re-test reliability. Where the data were qualitative, researchers typically reported inter-rater reliability on the classification of the children's responses. Findings suggest it is possible to develop an instrument with good psychometric properties for use by children aged six plus; there is however little evidence on instruments developed for use by younger children.

The extent to which children's evaluations are similar to the evaluations of parents raises important questions about validity. It can be assumed that perceptions should be different, but in the area of child and family practice differences in perception of the help received can indicate that the underlying cause of the difficulty remains untreated. In family therapy work it is crucial to try to understand everyone's point of view whilst not colluding with the family system producing symptomatic behaviour in an individual. In the case of a child this can result in symptom deterioration reinforcing parental perceptions that it is the child who has the problem. Or such a consequence can produce a resistance from the child at an older age to engaging with further help, thereby contributing to the development of mental health problems into adulthood.

It is important to explore the extent to which services are meeting the needs of differing groups of children in terms of age, gender, ethnicity, religion, and socio-economic status. The research on the relationship between client satisfactions in mental health services is better developed than in any other service sector. Three types of outcome have been used; client-assessed, parent-assessed, and therapist-assessed. There are inconsistent findings reported for the relationship between client satisfaction and therapist evaluation of treatment progress. The problem of practitioner power and status is regarded as influential in determining the ability of children and young people to express discontent with help offered. It is recognised that children and young people feel under pressure to say what they expect the practitioner to hear. In the context of family

therapy work practitioners need to recognise that children's views can be obscured or implicitly silenced by a combination of vulnerability due to their ascribed role as 'the problem', a fear of professionals with the power to punish, and a therapeutic stance that tries to equalise all members of the family. Enabling children and young people to express themselves in such oppressive environments is crucial.

A few studies have looked at the relationship with personal and family variables. Understanding these relationships is potentially important for understanding the way in which services may or may not be meeting the needs of various clients. The information currently available is limited. There have been relatively small numbers of attempts to do this and those that have, used different measures. It is now acknowledged at central government level that children from different socio-economic backgrounds may have differential access to or different expectations from services, but to date these possibilities have not been further explored (Audit Commission, 1999).

Age is a particularly important variable because of the different cognitive, social and emotional needs and abilities of children of different ages. Although individual studies differed in whether younger or older clients were more satisfied, a sufficient number of studies reported a moderate or high correlation between age and satisfaction/dissatisfaction (Shapiro et al., 1997). Only a small number of studies explored the relationship between gender and satisfaction but the evidence suggests no general tendency for greater satisfaction to be associated with either boys or girls. A more useful approach may be to explore the relationship between client/staff gender combinations (Bernzweig et al., 1997). In other words great care needs to be taken to select the most appropriate form of evidence gathering that is likely to produce a more valid response from a diverse population of children and young people. What works with a group of teenage clients may not work with a group of under 10s, or it may work but not with mixed gender groups.

There is very little evidence in many studies to demonstrate what impact their findings had on service development or practitioner attitudes and skills. In other words the research must lead to a positive impact on the way help and support are provided. Kalnins et al. (1992) argue that a shift in thinking is required from perceiving children and young people as recipients of health promotion efforts on their behalf, to accepting children and young people as active participants in the whole process. Another gap in the literature is the limited information on how children and young people felt about being asked their views on the service that they had received.

Some children may feel perturbed by this while others are enthusiastic about being given the opportunity to be part of a reflective process. It is a reasonable assumption that in the case of children and young people, those keenest to contribute are likely to reflect a positive perception of the service whereas those least keen reflect a negative experience. It is important for practitioners and researchers to continue to develop creative and flexible methods for enabling representative contributions from all those receiving the same service. It is a truism that we learn more from what went wrong than what went right.

Including children

Few studies have been undertaken with regard to therapeutic interventions with children and young people and whether they found the therapy helpful. Those undertaken have found that generally children speak less than parents when interviewed together. Adolescents express themselves in limited ways tending to agree or disagree, while therapists spoke more often to parents than to children when attempting to evaluate the help and support offered (Marshal et al., 1989; Friedlander et al., 1985; Mas et al., 1985; Cederborg, 1997). The question is whether this reflects a generalisable aversion to participating in research of this nature or whether the research design militates against inclusion and active participation. It also highlights the problem in family therapy work of ensuring that children and young people are able to genuinely participate in expressing views and feelings.

Practitioners have built up a repertoire of therapeutic methods in working with children and young people, engaging with them in areas

of great sensitivity such as bereavement, parental separation, or sexual abuse. The same repertoire of research techniques is yet to be developed to ensure that children and young people are being given the best possible chance of contributing to service evaluation. Evidence of children's desire to be part of therapy suggests that children's reactions to therapy can be influenced by their attachment style (Smith et al., 1996; Strickland Clark et al., 2000). In families where there are insecure attachments for example, children can feel constrained to speak more freely because of fears of what the consequences might be and the discomfort in exposing painful or difficult feelings. Ways to engage such children have been developed and could be adapted by researchers.

This poses important challenges for practitioners and researchers wanting to research in areas where there are factors likely to inhibit participation. Given the central position that attachment theory occupies in much training it should not be too difficult for staff to incorporate this dimension as we saw in Chapter 6 in evaluating family therapy intervention. The alternative is to automatically exclude some children and young people and miss the opportunity to gather valuable evidence to improve service provision rather than designing strategies to overcome these difficulties.

There has been a tendency in approaches to facilitate communication with children to favour those which are standardised and produce quantifiable results (McGurk, 1992). Williamson and Butler (1996) note that there is a full literature about observational techniques but little that addresses qualitative approaches. There is nevertheless, an emerging trend to move towards emphasising children's competencies and strengths in being able to describe their own perceptions (Mayall, 1994).

There is little guidance available in the research literature about conversational methods with children. Even child psychology texts concentrate on experimental, observational and standard measurement techniques (Vasta, Haith and Miller, 1993). Children in interview situations are affected by the perceived power and status of adults and by presumptions about what answers are expected (Garbarino Stott and Erikson Institute, 1992). The combination of adult assumptions about children and young persons competence in contributing to service evaluation, together with children and young persons assumptions about adult power and authority, conspire to hinder meaningful developments to improve the situation.

Ethical considerations

In seeking to ascertain the perceptions of children and young people about family therapy the primary ethical consideration is to prevent any harm or wrongdoing during the process of research. While respecting children's competencies researchers need to also fulfil their responsibilities to protect children and young people. A more social-anthropological approach that allows data to be co-produced in the relationship between researchers and researched, rather than being driven by problem-oriented adult questions is more appropriate because it permits the building up of information on the general topic over time.

There is considerable uncertainty about the issue of children's consent to participate in research. The issue has yet to be fully tested in court. This is linked to consent for treatment which has been affected by the decision of the House of Lords in 1985 (Gillick 3 All ER) ruling that competent children under 16 years of age can consent. Since then further court cases have modified the Gillick principle so that if either the child or any person with parental responsibility gives consent to treatment, doctors can proceed, even if one or more of these people, including the child, disagree. While these rulings do not strictly apply to research they have implications for children's rights.

Parents may have to sign the research consent form until their child is 16 or 18 for medical research. But non-invasive social and educational research may not require parental consent because of the lack of harm. Social research requiring answers to questions implies consent if the subject co-operates. But is a child co-operating under pressure, afraid to decline or to challenge adult authority figures? It is argued that the onus should be on the adults to prove that the child does not

have the capacity to decide, and the safest route is to ask for parental consent as well as the children's, when they are able to understand (Alderson, 1995). In the context of child and family work the concept of informed consent requires sensitive explanation of the nature and purpose of research clearly and unambiguously. At the very least it should allow for informed dissent from the children and young people themselves (Morrow and Richards, 1996).

There is little evidence of researchers actively involving children to select topics, plan research or advise on monitoring research. Where this has been done the results demonstrate that young people value being asked to participate in this way, and have much to offer the development of the research process. It has been established that using teenagers as researchers with other young people, for instance, has certain advantages over using adult researchers (Alderson, 1995). Properly supported and trained they can engage with younger children in ways adults are unable to achieve. The timing of research with children and young people, feedback to them, and the dissemination of findings, are further topics for ethical consideration. Attempting to interview during the course of intervention could be invasive or undermining of the therapeutic or supportive work being undertaken. Gaining access to the children and young people after the problem has been resolved could be hampered by a need for the child and family to put their experiences behind them and avoid being reminded of painful issues.

Ethically the findings should be fedback to participants but in practice the time delay between data collection and writing up, together with access to children and young people militate against achieving this aim.

Dissemination of the findings and the use to which they are put by service managers or government departments presents a clear responsibility to researchers to ensure that the views and perceptions of the children and young people are not misrepresented or distorted. Children as a powerless group in society are not able to challenge the ways in which research findings about them are presented (Thomas and O'Kane, 1998; Walker, 2003a).

Attempts to gain research evidence from children and young people demonstrate that practitioners and researchers are adopting a wide variety of methods, techniques, and approaches to the difficult task of engaging children and young people. The number of studies is relatively small compared with studies of adult populations. This highlights a gap in the evidence base required on which to base judgments about service and practitioner development. Government policy in this area is designed to produce more accessible, acceptable and appropriate services (Audit Commission, 1999).

It is important to draw attention to the significance of the emotional impact such research has and suggests ways of encompassing the effects of research into the research design. The increasing trend towards including children and young people as active, rather than passive recipients of health and social care means that the task of developing robust methods for obtaining children's and young peoples' perceptions is important. Enabling them to collaborate in the design of research studies and to be consulted fully about the areas they consider important to research can only enrich these studies. The impact such research has in terms of the immediate effect on the child or young person, and on later service and practitioner development, are areas requiring attention from researchers involved in this area of work.

Children are not a homogenous group. The age ranges from childhood to adolescence incorporates several developmental stages which would suggest attention being paid to the design of developmentally-appropriate methods. A variety of participatory research methods are being developed including the use of mapping and modelling, diagrams, drawing and collage, drama and puppetry. These methods are designed to empower children and young people by enabling them to represent their own situations, to reflect on their experiences and to influence change (Chambers, 1997). Gender differences are considered important in terms of children and young people's perceptions in other areas of life experience, therefore attention needs to be paid to considering the gender dimension in research studies. This means considering the advantages and potential disadvantages of using male or female researchers. Children and young people from black and other ethnic minorities have experiences conditioned by racism and other social disadvantages, which should be incorporated in research. This might for instance mean employing black and other ethnic minority staff to conduct more enabling research.

There is growing evidence of the desire from children and young people to be involved in decisions and services affecting their lives. There is equally evidence of a response from a number of researchers and practitioners to incorporate children and young person's perceptions in service evaluation. Further research is indicated to contribute to the refinement of methodologies, to improve reliability and to increase participation of children and young people as recipients of family therapy in order to enhance service quality and development.

Change and the practice evidence base

Central to an empowering socially inclusive approach in work with children and families is finding out whether the work has contributed towards the process of change. Change can be considered as something that is endless, constant and inevitable. How it is perceived and experienced by service users is crucial. Various models of family therapy intervention permit change stemming from within the psyche of the person to physical changes in their environment and abilities (Walker, 2003c).

There are changes imposed on certain clients compulsorily and those that are accepted voluntarily, either of which may lead to long-term benefits for them or their kin. Change is often thought of as something initiated by a practitioner in a linear cause-and-effect process. But it can be more useful to think about it in a more circular or reflexive pattern using systems theory as an explanatory model. How much did the practitioner change during the course of an intervention? What impact did the client have on them and how did this affect their thinking and behaviour? Indeed most of the change may occur within the practitioner themselves as they find out more over time about a family and their circumstances compared to the first encounter.

Change is connected to difference but every stakeholder in the change process has a unique perception of what counts as difference. Pointing out differences to a family might be experienced as empowering but it might equally provoke feelings of fear or anxiety. A minimum amount of help might produce significant changes and equally a substantial amount of intervention results in no change or a worsening of circumstances. Where a practitioner chooses to look for change may not be where other professionals or the family is looking. Change can therefore be liberating or constraining, it can generate enlightenment or promote feelings of anger, loss and bereavement. Maintaining a degree of professional optimism with realism and managing uncertainty with a modest and respectful approach offers practitioners the potential for being a useful resource to their clients.

The need to expand and refine the evidence base of practice in order to demonstrate effectiveness is more important than ever especially in work with children and families (Walker, 2003). The growing problems faced by families requires a concerted effort from all agencies in contact with children and young people to understand the services they are providing and finding out better ways of measuring success. Three key factors have been identified in defining and explaining why evidence-based practice is not an option, but a necessity (Sheldon and Chilvers, 2000):

Conscientiousness – this means a constant vigilance to monitor and review practice and to maintain service user welfare as paramount. It entails keeping up-to-date with new developments and a commitment to further professional understanding of human growth and development and social problems.

Explicitness – this means working with clients in an open and honest way, based on reliable evidence of what works and what is understood to be effective. The principle of explicitness demands a review of the available options with clients based upon thorough assessment of their problems.

Judiciousness – this means the exercise of sound, prudent, sensible, judgment. Potential

risks arising from some, or no intervention either in cases or policies, should be thoroughly assessed and evaluated in the knowledge that not all eventualities can be predicted.

The drive to encourage research-minded professions in order to improve practice standards and accountability is however in danger of producing a confusion of research studies varying in quality and methodological rigour yet producing potentially useful data hidden within the quantity being produced. Practitioner research is being encouraged as a means of influencing policy, management and practice using evaluative concepts moulded by service-user expectations (Fuller, 1996). In the context of a range of practice situations, practitioners can contribute to good quality effectiveness and evaluation studies by working in partnership with individuals and families to ensure their perspectives are at the heart of this activity.

The broader view

One of the significant conclusions to be drawn from considering the wider role of Family Support in contemporary practice is the impressive amount of activity, the variation in methods of intervention, and the worrying lack of systematic review of available research findings on which to build a reliable evidence base (Chalmers, 1994; Webb, 2001). Practitioner research is being encouraged as a means of influencing European social policy, management, and practice, using evaluative concepts moulded by service-user expectations (Fuller, 1996; Walker, 2001a). By taking this broader rather than narrow view of research you can help contribute to social policy changes that will ultimately impact on your services and thus benefit families in a circular process.

There is evidence that research into children's perceptions as recipients of family support services that focus on competence and resources, rather than problems or deviance, helps provide a fuller picture of their circumstances and highlights the importance of the personal relationship established with their practitioner or counsellor (Sandbaek, 1999). It is also consistent with the right under the terms of the UN Charter to be consulted with and to express their views about, services provided for them (UN, 1989). The implications seem to be that by enlarging the focus of effectiveness measures it is possible to see children not just with problems but also as having positive and constructive elements in their family lives and building on these and amplifying them wherever possible.

This view is echoed in recommendations based on thorough research into interventions targeted at the child, teacher and parent who demonstrate that the *combined effect* produces the most sustained reduction in conflict problems both at home and at school, and in peer relationships (Webster-Stratton, 1997). Recognising and building on the children's own perspectives provides new opportunities for work with children and families guided by possibilities adults are not aware of or fail to pay enough attention to.

Creating acceptable, accessible, and appropriate family support, for every family which requires it, means acknowledging the poor general health of ethnic minority families attributable to their impoverished socio-economic circumstances and the impact of personal and institutional racism. Clifford (1998) offers a useful model for consideration of an anti-oppressive assessment framework which takes into account social divisions. Further research with ethnic minority families to investigate effectiveness is required to build on the limited work undertaken (Trevino, 1999). The needs of gay and lesbian families are virtually absent in the literature on family support which reflect homophobic and discriminatory practices in health and social care generally. This gap needs to be filled on the grounds of equality and to ensure appropriate support can be offered to every family, however it is defined, and to enable different parenting practices to be valued and learned from (Salmon and Hall, 1999; Eliason, 1996).

Research suggests that family support programmes tend to focus on a single outcome as a measure of success such as changes in the child's behaviour, rather than taking into account other dimensions such as improved parent/child interactions or use of community resources (Gardner, 1998). This reflects the problem-oriented rather than solution-oriented texture to much of the literature and a narrow, rather than broad field of vision such as that provided in family therapy practice. There is evidence of a renaissance in Britain of specific family support work focussed on children's behavioural and emotional needs and emerging mental health problems, as well as prevention of harm. The evidence suggests it is developing largely outside statutory services reflecting the trend in retrenchment of state welfare provision, and the expansion of voluntary, charitable, private, and community group activity where the research infrastructure is underdeveloped. This is a further impediment to discovering what works for which families in specific circumstances and can therefore be replicated with confidence based on reliable evidence.

Family Support in its widest definition is being provided through fiscal and social policy changes that do not easily yield short-term effectiveness measures. Together with government backing for the expansion of the voluntary sector to provide family support services, this combination represents a further narrowing of the definition of professional work and a missed opportunity to harness vital skills in assessment and intervention. Family therapy and systems theory offer a powerful way of conceptualising people's problems and a range of interventions to support them through the process of change. Used properly, these skills can complement the mosaic of diverse programmes of Family Support embracing enthusiastic voluntary activity, statutory child care, community care and mental health service provision that all, at some point, maintain the family as their primary focus of concern and intervention.

References and Further Reading

AAMFT (American Association for Marriage and Family Therapy) (1991). *AAMFT Code of Ethics*. Washington DC: Author.

Adams, A., Erath, P. and Shardlow, S. (2000) *Fundamentals of Social Work in Selected European Countries*. Lyme Regis, Russell House Publishing.

Adams, R., Dominelli, L. and Payne, M. (2002) *Critical Practice in Social Work*. Basingstoke, Palgrave.

Akister, J. (1998) Attachment Theory and Systemic Practice: Research update. *Journal of Family Therapy*, 20: 4, 353–366.

Akister, J. and Stevenson-Hinde, J. (1991) Identifying Families at Risk: Exploring the Potential of the McMaster Family Assessment Device. *Journal of Family Therapy*, 13: 411–421.

Alderson P. et al. (1996) *What Works: Effective Social Interventions in Child Welfare*. Barkingside, Barnardos.

Alderson, P. (1995) *Listening to Children. Children Ethics and Social Research*. Barkingside, Barnardos.

Alderson, P. (2000) *Young People's Rights*. London, Jessica Kingsley.

Anderson, H. (1997) *Conversation, Language and Possibilities: a Postmodern Approach to Therapy*. New York, Basic Books.

Anderson, H. (2001) Postmodern Collaborative and Person centred Therapies: What would Carl Rogers say? *Journal of Family Therapy*, 23: 339–360.

Anderson, T. (1990) *The Reflecting Team*. New York, WW Norton.

Arcelus, J., Bellerby, T. and Vostanis, V. (1999) A Mental Health Service for Young People in the Care of the Local Authority. *Clinical Child Psychology and Psychiatry*, 4: 2, 233–245.

Archambault, R., Doherty, M., and Bishop, D. S. (1990) *Parent and Clinician Perceptions of Family Functioning*. Paper presented at the First International Conference of the McMaster Model of Family Functioning. Providence RI.

Audit Commission. (1998) *Child and Adolescent Mental Health Services*. London, HMSO.

Audit Commission. (1999) *Children in Mind*. London, HMSO.

Audit Commission (2000) *Another Country: Implementing Dispersal Under the Immigration and Asylum Act 1999*. London, HMSO.

Bagley, C. and Mallick, K. (1995) Negative Self perception and Components of Stress in Canadian, British and Hong Kong adolescents. *Perceptual Motor Skills*. 81: 123–127.

Bagley, C. and Mallick, K. (2000) How Adolescents perceive their Emotional Life, Behaviour, and Self-esteem in Relation to Family Stressors: a Six-culture Study. In: Singh, N., Leung, J. and Singh, A. *International Perspectives on Child and Adolescent Mental Health*. Oxford, Elsevier.

Baradon, T., Sinason, V. and Yabsley, S. (1999) Assessment of Parents and Young Children: a Child Psychotherapy Point of View. *Child Care Health and Development*, 25: 137–153.

Barber, C.E. and Lyness, K.P. (2001) Ethical Issues in Family Care of Older People with Dementia: Implications for Family Therapists. *Home Health Care Services Quarterly*, 20: 3, 1–26.

Barber, J.G. and Deffabbro, P. (2000) *Research in Social Work Practice*, 10: 2, 243–256.

Barker, P. (1998) *Basic Family Therapy*. Blackwells Science.

Barlow, J. (1998) Parent Training Programmes and Behaviour Problems: Findings from a Systematic Review. In: Buchanan, A. and Hudson, B. (Eds.) *Parenting, Schooling, and Children's Behaviour: Interdisciplinary Approaches*. Alton. Ashgate Publishers.

Barnes, C. (1991) *Disabled People in Britain and Discrimination*. London, Hurst.

Barnes, C. and Mercer, G. (1997) *Doing Disability Research*. Leeds, The Disability Press.

Barnes, H., Thornton, P. and Maynard, S. (1998) *Disabled People and Employment: A Review of Research and Development Work*. Bristol, Policy Press.

Barnes, M. and Warren, L. (1999) *Paths to Empowerment*. Bristol, Policy Press.

BASW (2002) *Code of Ethics for Social Workers*. Birmingham, BASW.

Barry, M. and Hallett, C. (1998) *Social Exclusion and Social Work*. Lyme Regis, Russell House Publishing.

Bateson, G. (1973) *Steps to an Ecology of Mind*. St Albans, Paladin.

Bayley, R. (1998) *Transforming Children's Lives: the Importance of Early Intervention*. London, Family Policy Studies Centre.

Beckett, C. and Wrighton, E. (2000) What Matters to Me is Not What You're Talking About: Maintaining the Social Model of Disability in Public Private Negotiations. *Disability and Society*. 15: 7, 991–999.

Bell, J. (1961) *Family Group Therapy, Public Health Monograph no 64*. Washington DC, US Government Printing Office.

Belsky, J., Campbell, S.B., Cohn, J.F. and Moore, G. (1996) Instability of Infant-Parent Attachment Stability. *Developmental Psychology*, 32: 921–924.

Bentovim, A. and Bingley Miller, L. (2002) *The Family Assessment*. DoH, Pavilion.

Bentovim, A., Gorrell Barnes, G. and Cooklin, A. (Eds.) (1982) *Family Therapy: Complementary Frameworks of Theory and Practice*. London, Academic Press.

Berg, I.K. and Jaya, A. (1993) Different and Same: Family Therapy with American-Asian Families. *Journal of Marital and Family Therapy*, 19: 1, 31–39.

Berg, I.M. (1991) *Family Preservation: A Brief Therapy Workbook*. London, BT Press.

Berger, M. and Jurkovic, G. (1984) *Practising Family Therapy in Diverse Settings*. San Francisco, Jossey-Bass.

Bernzweig, J., Takayama, J., Phibbs, C., Lewis, C. and Pantell, R.H. (1997) Gender Differences in Physician-patient Communication. *Archives of Pediatric Adolescent Medicine*. 151: 586–591.

Bhugra, D. and Bahl, V. (1999). *Ethnicity: An Agenda for Mental Health*. London, Gaskell.

Bhugra, D. (1999) *Mental Health of Ethnic Minorities*. London, Gaskell.

Bhui, K. and Olajide, D. (1999) *Mental Health Service Provision for a Multi-Cultural Society*. London, Saunders.

Bishop, D.S. and Miller, I.W. (1988) Traumatic Brain Injury: Empirical Family Assessment Techniques. *Journal of Head Trauma Rehabilitation*, 3: 4, 16–30.

Bishop, M.D., Epstein, N.B., Keitner, G.I., Miller, I.W. and Zlotnick, C. (1987) *McMaster Structured Interview of Family Functioning (McSIFF)*. Unpublished Manuscript, Brown University, Providence, R. I.

Bochner, S. (1994) Cross-cultural Differences in the Self-concept: A test of Hofstede's Individualism/collectivism Distinction. *Journal of Cross-Cultural Psychology*. 2: 273–283.

Bourne, D. (1993) Over-chastisement, Child non-compliance and Parenting Skills: A Behavioural Intervention by a Family Centre Social Worker. *British Journal of Social Work*. 5: 481–500.

Bowlby, J. (1969) *Attachment and Loss (Vol. 1)*. London, Hogarth.

Bowlby, J. (1979) *The Making and Breaking of Affectional Bonds*. Tavistock Publications.

Braye, S. and Preston-Shoot, M. (1995) *Empowering Practice in Social Care*. Buckingham, Open University Press.

Bretherton, I. (1985) Attachment Theory: Retrospect and Prospect. *Monographs of the Society for Research in Child Development*, 50: 1–2, (209), 3–35.

Brown, B., Crawford, P. and Darongkamas, J. (2000) Blurred Roles and Permeable Boundaries: the Experience of Multi-disciplinary

Working in Community Mental Health. *Health and Social Care in the Community*. 8: 6, 425–435.

Brown, J.H. and Christensen, D.N. (1999) *Family Therapy Theory and Practice*. 2nd edn, London, International Thompson.

Burkemper, E.M. (2002) Family Therapists' Ethical Decision-Making Processes In Two Duty-To-Warn Situations. *Journal of Marital and Family Therapy*, 28: 2, 203–212.

Burnham, J. (1986) Family Therapy: First Steps towards a Systemic Approach. London, Routledge.

Byng-Hall, J. (1998) *Rewriting Family scripts – Improvisation and Systems Change*. New York, Guilford Press.

Calder, M. (2004) The Assessment Framework: A Critique and Reformulation. In: *Assessments in Child Care: A Comprehensive Guide to Frameworks and their Use*. Lyme Regis, Russell House Publishing.

Campbell, D. and Draper, R. (1985) *Applications of Systemic Family Therapy*. London, Grune and Stratton.

Cannan, C., Berry, L. and Lyons, K. (1992) *Social Work and Europe*. London, Macmillan/BASW.

Capra, F. (1997) *The Web of Life: A New Synthesis of Mind and Matter*. London, Flaming.

Carr, A. (2000) *What Works with Children and Adolescents?* London, Routledge.

Carter, B. and McGoldrick, M. (1999) *The Expanded Family Life Cycle: Individual, Family and Social Perspectives*. 3rd edn, Boston, Allyn and Bacon.

Cederborg, A. (1997) Young Children's Participation in Family Therapy talk. *The American Journal of Family Therapy*, 25: 28–38.

Chalmers, I. (1994) Assembling the Evidence. In: Alderson et al. *What Works? Effective Social Interventions in Child Welfare*. Barkingside. Barnardos.

Chambers, R. (1997) *Whose Reality Counts? Putting the First Last*. London, Intermediate Technology.

Cheetham, J., Fuller, R., McIvor, G. and Petch, A. (1992) *Evaluating Social Work Effectiveness*. Buckingham, Open University Press.

Christiansen, E. and James, G. (Eds.) (2000) *Research with Children, Perspectives and Practices*. London, Falmer Press.

Clarke, N. (2001) The Impact of In-service Training within Social Services. *British Journal of Social Work*. 31: 757–774.

Clifford, D. (1998) *Social Assessment Theory and Practice*. Aldershot, Aldgate Publishing.

Cohen, J. C., Coyne, J. and Duvall, J. (1993) Adopted and Biological Children in the Clinic: Family, Parental and Child Characteristics. *Journal of Child Psychology and Psychiatry*, 34: 4, 545–562.

Cohn, D.A., Silver, D.H., Cowan, C.P. and Cowan, P.A. (1992) Working Models of Childhood Attachment and Couples' Relationships. *Journal of Family Issues*, 13: 432–449.

Coleman, M., Ganong, L. and Cable, S. (1997). Beliefs about Women's Intergenerational Family Obligations to Provide Support before and after Divorce and Remarriage. *Journal of Marriage and the Family*. 59: 1, 165–176.

Connelly, N. and Stubbs, P. (1997) *Trends in Social Work and Social Work Education across Europe*, London, NISW.

Cook, W. L. (2000) Understanding Attachment Security in Family Context. *Journal of Personality and Social Psychology*, 78: 2, 285–294.

Cooper, P. (Ed.) (1999) *Understanding and Supporting Children with Emotional and Behavioural Difficulties*. London, Jessica Kingsley.

Corker, M. (1999) New Disability Discourse, the Principle of Optimization and Social Change. In: Corker, M. and French, S. (Eds.) *Disability Discourse*. Buckingham, Open University Press.

Costner, R., Guttman, H., Sigal, J., Epstein, N. and Rakoff, V. (1971) Process and Outcome in Conjoint Family Therapy. *Family Process*. 10: 451–474.

Cote, G.L. (1997) Socio-economic Attainment, Regional Disparities, and Internal Migration. *European Sociological Review*, 13: 1, 55–77.

Crawford, M. and Kessel, A. (1999) Not Listening to Patients: The Use and Misuse of Patient Satisfaction Studies. *International Journal of Social Psychiatry*. 45: 1, 1–6.

Crisp, S. (1994) *Counting on Families: Social Audit Report on the Provision of Family Support Services*. London, Exploring Parenthood.

Crittenden, P.M. (1999) Danger and Development: The Organization of Self-protective Strategies. In Vondra, J. and Barnett, D. (Eds.)

Monographs for the Society for Research on Child Development. 3: 258, 64.

Czaja, S.J. and Rubert, M.P. (2002) Telecommunications Technology as an Aid to Family Caregivers of Persons with Dementia. *Psychosomatic Medicine*, 64: 3, 469–476.

Daines, R., Lyon, K. and Parsloe, P. (1990) *Aiming for Partnership*. London. Barnardos.

Dallos, R. and Draper, R. (2000) *An Introduction to Family Therapy*. Buckingham, Open University Press.

Davis, A. and Ellis, K. (1995) Enforced Altruism or Community care? In: Hugman, R. and Smith, D. (Eds.) *Ethical Issues in Social Work*. London. Routledge.

Davis, H., Sourr, P., Cox, A., Lynch, M., Von Roenne, A. and Hahn, K. (1997) A Description and Evaluation of a Community Child Mental Health Service. *Clinical Child Psychology and Psychiatry*, 2: 2, 221–238.

Davis, J., Rendell, P. and Sims, D. (1999) The Joint Practitioner – a New Concept in Professional Training. *Journal of Interprofessional Care*.13: 4, 395–404.

De Shazer, (1982) *Patterns of Brief Therapy: An Ecosystemic Approach*. New York, Guilford Press.

Debell, D, and Everett, G. (1997) *In a Class Apart: A Study of School Nursing*. Norwich. East Norfolk Health Authority.

DeBell, D. and Walker, S. (2002) *Evaluation of the Family Support Service in Norfolk CAMHS*. Cambridge, Anglia Polytechnic University.

Dennis, J. and Smith, T. (2002) Nationality, Immigration and Asylum Bill 2002: its Impact on Children, *Childright*, 187: 16–17.

Department for Education and Employment (1998) *Towards an Interdisciplinary Framework for Developing Work with Children and Young People*. *Childhood Studies Discipline Network*. Conference presentation: Cambridge, Robinson College.

Department of Health (1989) *The Children Act*. London, HMSO.

Department of Health (1995) *Child Protection: Messages from Research*. London, HMSO.

Department of Health (1997a) *Developing Partnerships in Mental Health*. London, HMSO.

Department of Health (1997b) *General Household Survey*. London, HMSO.

Department of Health (1997c) *Innovations Fund Grant*. London, HMSO.

Department of Health (1997d) *The New NHS: Modern, Dependable*. London, HMSO.

Department of Health (1998a) *Disabled Children: Directions for their Future Care*. London, HMSO.

Department of Health (1998b) *Modernising Mental Health Services: Safe, Supportive and Sensible*. London, HMSO.

Department of Health (1998c) *Partnership in Action*. London, HMSO.

Department of Health (1998d) *Modernising Social Services*. London, HMSO.

Department of Health (1999a) *Quality Protects programme: Transforming Children's Services 2000–01*. LAC circular. (99) 33. London, HMSO.

Department of Health (1999b) *The Health Act*. London, HMSO.

Department of Health (2000) *Framework for the Assessment of Children in Need*. London, HMSO.

Department of Health/SSI (2000a) *A Quality Strategy for Social Care*. London, HMSO.

Department of Health (2000b) *The Children Act Report 1995–1999*. London, HMSO.

Department of Health (2001) *Making it Work: Inspection of Welfare to Work for Disabled People*. London, HMSO.

Department of Health and Department for Education and Employment (1996) *Children's Service Planning: Guidance for Inter-Agency Working*. London, HMSO.

DfES (2003) *Every Child Matters*. London, HMSO.

Dimigen, G., Del Priore, C., Butler, S., Evans, S., Ferguson, L. and Swan, M. (1999) Psychiatric Disorder among Children at Time of Entering Local Authority Care. *British Medical Journal*. 319: 675–676.

Dogra, N., Parkin, A., Gale, F. and Frake, C. (2002) *A Multi-disciplinary Handbook of Child and Adolescent Mental Health for Front-line Professionals*. London, Jessica Kingsley.

Doherty, W. and Beaton, J. (2000) Family Therapists, Community and Civil Renewal. *Family Process*. 39: 149–159.

Dominelli, L. (1988) *Anti-Racist Social Work*. Basingstoke, Macmillan.

Dominelli, L. (1996) Deprofessionalising Social Work: Equal Opportunities, Competences, and Postmodernism. *British Journal of Social Work*. 26: 2, 153–175.

Dominelli, L. (2002) *Anti-Oppressive Social Work: Theory and Practice*. Basingstoke, Palgrave Macmillan.

Dominelli, L. (Ed) (1999) *Community Approaches to Child Welfare*. Aldershot, Ashgate.

Donovan, M. (2003) Mind the Gap: the Need for a Generic Bridge between Psychoanalytic and Systemic Approaches. *Journal of Family Therapy*, 25: 115–135.

Douglas, T. (2000) *Basic Groupwork*. 2nd edn. London, Routledge.

Dryden, W. (1988) *Family Therapy in Britain*. Milton Keynes, OU Press.

Dunn, J. (1995) *From One Child to Two*. London, Ballantine Books.

Durlak, J. (1998) Primary Prevention Programmes for Children and Adolescents are Effective. *Journal of Mental Health*. 7: 5, 454–469.

Dwivedi, K.N. (2002) *Meeting the Needs of Ethnic Minority Children*. 2nd edn, London, Jessica Kingsley.

Eayrs, C. and Jones, R. (1992) Methodological Issues and Future Directions in the Evaluation of Early Intervention Programmes. *Child Care, Health and Development*. 18: 15–28.

Eber, L., Osuch, R. and Redditt, C. (1996)) School-based Applications of the Wraparound Process: Early Results on Service Provision and Student Outcomes. *Journal of Child and Family Studies*. 5: 83–99.

Eliason, M. (1996) Lesbian and Gay Family Issues. *Journal of Family Nursing*. 2: 1, 10–29.

Elliot, R. and Shapiro, D. (1992) Client and Therapists as Analysts of Significant Events. In: onkmanian, S.G. and Rennie, D. (Eds.) *Psychotherapy Process Research, Paradigmatic Narrative Approaches*. Newbury Park, CA, Sage.

Epstein, N.B. and Bishop, D.S. (1981) Problem-Centred Systems Therapy of the Family. In: Gurman, A.S. and Kniskern, D.P. (Eds.) *Handbook of Family Therapy*. Brunner/Mazel.

Epstein, N.B., Baldwin, L.M. and Bishop, D.S. (1983) The McMaster Family Assessment Device. *Journal of Marital and Family Therapy*, 9: 2, 171–180.

Epstein, N.B., Bishop, D.S. and Levine, S. (1978) The McMaster Model of Family Functioning. *Journal of Marriage and Family Counselling*, 4: 19–31.

Estrada, A. and Pinsof, W. (1995) The Effectiveness of Family Therapies for Selected Behaviour Disorders of Childhood, *Journal of Marital and Family Therapy*, 21: 4, 403–440.

Everitt, A. and Hardiker, P. (1996) *Evaluating Good Practice*. Basingstoke, Macmillan.

Fagin, C. M. (1992) Collaboration between Nurses and Physicians; No Longer a Choice. *Academic Medicine*. 67: 5, 295–303.

Falicov, C. (1995) Training to Think Culturally: a Multi-dimensional Comparative Framework. *Family Process*, 34: 373–388.

Falloon, I. and Fadden, G. (1995) *Integrated Mental Health Care: a Comprehensive Community-based Approach*. Cambridge, Cambridge University Press.

Farrington, D. (1995) The Development of Offending and Antisocial Behaviour From Childhood: Key Findings From the Cambridgeshire Study in Delinquent Development. *Journal of Child Psychology and Psychiatry*.

Fawcett, B. (2000) Look, Listen and Learn. *Community Care*. July 27. 24–25.

Feeney, B.C. and Collins, (2001) Predictors of Caregiving in Adult Intimate Relationships: An Attachment Theoretical Perspective. *Journal of Personality and Social Psychology*, 80: 6, 972–994.

Feeney, J.A. (2003) The Systemic Nature of Couple Relationships: An Attachment Perspective. In Erdman, P. and Caffery, T. *Attachment and Family Systems*. New York and Hove, Brunner Routledge.

Fernando, S. (2002) *Mental Health Race and Culture*. Basingstoke, Palgrave.

Finch, J. (1987) The Vignette Technique in Survey Research. *Sociology*. 21: 1, 105–114.

Firth, M., Dyer, M. and Wilkes, J. (1999) Reducing the Distance: Mental Health Social Work in General Practice. *Journal of Interprofessional Care*, 13: 4, 335–344.

Fletcher-Campbell, F. (2001) Issues of Inclusion. *Emotional and Behavioural Difficulties*. 6: 2, 69–89.

Freeman, I., Morrison, A., Lockhart, F. and Swanson, M. (1996) Consulting Service Users:

the Views of Young People. In: Hill, M. and Aldgate, J. (Eds.) *Child Welfare Services: Developments in Law, Policy, Practice and Research.* London, Jessica Kingsley.

Freeman, J., Epston, D. and Lobovits, D. (1997) *Playful Approaches to Serious Problems: Narrative Therapy with Children and their Families.* New York, Norton.

Friedlander, M., Highlen, P. and Lassiter, W. (1985) Content Analytic Comparison of Four Expert Counsellors' Approaches to Family Treatment. *Journal of Counselling Psychology,* 32: 171–180.

Friedlander, M.L. (2001) Family Therapy Research: Science into Practice, Practice into Science. In: Nichols, M.P. and Schwartz, R.C. (Eds.) *Family Therapy: Concepts and Methods.* 5th edn, Boston, Alleyn and Bacon.

Fristad, M.A. (1989) A Comparison of the McMaster and Circumplex Family Assessment Instruments. *Journal of Marital and Family Therapy,* 15: 259–269.

Fuchs, D. (1995) Preserving and Strengthening Families and Protecting Children: Social Network Intervention, a Balanced Approach to the Prevention of Child Maltreatment. In: Hudson, J. and Galway, B. (Eds.) *Child Welfare in Canada: Research and Policy Implications.* Toronto, Thomson Educational Publishing.

Fuller, R. (1996) Evaluating Social Work Effectiveness: a Pragmatic Approach. In:

Garbarino, J., Stott, F. and Erikson Institute (1992) *What Children Can Tell Us.* San Francisco, Jossey-Bass.

Gardner, R. (1998) *Family Support: Practitioners Guide.* BASW. Birmingham, Venture Press.

Ghate, D. and Daniels, A. (1997) *Talking about my Generation.* London, NSPCC.

Gibbons, J, and Wilding, J. (1995) *Needs, Risks and Family Support Plans: Social Services Departments' Responses to Neglected Children.* Norwich, University of East Anglia.

Gibson-Cline, J. (Ed.) (1996) *Adolescence: From Crisis to Coping.* London, Butterworth-Heinemann.

Gillick v Wisbech and W Norfolk AHA. (1986). AC112.

Glantz, M.D. and Johnson, J.L. (1999) *Resilience and Development: Positive Life Adaptations.* New York, Plenum.

Goldenberg, I. and Goldenberg, H. (2004) *Family Therapy: an Overview.* Pacific Grove, CA, Thomson Learning.

Goldner, V. (1985) Feminism and Family Therapy. *Family Process.* 24: 31–47.

Goldner, V. (1991) Sex, Power and Gender: a Feminist Analysis of the Politics of Passion. *Journal of Feminist Family Therapy,* 3: 63–83.

Goodman, R. and Scott, S. (1997) *Child Psychiatry.* London, Sage.

Gordon, G. and Grant, R. (1997) *How We Feel: An Insight into the Emotional World of Teenagers.* London, Jessica Kingsley.

Gorell-Barnes, G. (1984) *Working with Families.* Basingstoke, Macmillan/BASW.

Gorell-Barnes, G. (1998) *Family Therapy in Changing Times.* Basingstoke, Macmillan.

Greenbaum, T. (1987) *The Practical Handbook and Guide to Focus Group Research.* Lexington, USA, Lexington Books.

Griffiths, R. (1998) *Educational Citizenship and Independent Learning.* London, Jessica Kingsley.

Gross, D., Fogg, L. and Tucker, S. (1995) The Efficacy of Parent Training for Promoting Positive Parent–Toddler Relationships. *Research in Nursing and Health.* 18: 489–499.

Gurman, A. and Kniskern, D. (Eds.) (1991) *Handbook of Family Therapy Vol 2.* New York, Brunner/Mazell.

Hague, G. (2000) *Reducing Domestic Violence: What works?* PRCU Briefing Note, London, HMSO.

Haley, J. (1976) *Problem Solving Therapy.* San Francisco, Jossey-Bass.

Hardiker, P. (1995) *The Social Policy Contexts of Services to Prevent Unstable Family Life.* York, Joseph Rowntree Foundation.

Hardy, K. and Laszloffy, T. (1994) Deconstructing Race in Family Therapy. *Journal of Feminist Family Therapy.* 3: 4, 5–33.

Hare-Mustin R. (1978) A Feminist Approach to Family Therapy. *Family Process.* 17: 181–194.

Hare-Mustin, R. (1991) Sex, Lies and Headaches: the Problem is Power. *Journal of Feminist Family Therapy,* 3: 39–61.

Harrington, R. (1997) The Role of the Child and Adolescent Mental Health Service in Preventing Later Depressive Disorder: Problems and Prospects. *Child Psychology and Psychiatry Review.* 2: 2, 46–57.

Hasselkus, B.R. (1991) Ethical Dilemmas in Family Caregiving for the Elderly: Implications for Occupational Therapy. *The American Journal of Occupational Therapy*, 45: 206–212.

Hazan, C. and Shaver, P.R. (1987) Romantic Love Conceptualised as an Attachment Process. *Journal of Personality and Social Psychology*, 52: 3, 511–524.

Hazel, N. (1995) *Seen and Heard: an Examination of Methods for Collecting Data from Young People. Social Research Update.* Guildford, University of Surrey.

Health Advisory Service (1995) *Together We Stand: Thematic Review on the Commissioning, Role, and Management of Child and Adolescent Mental Health Services.* London, HMSO.

Hellinckx, W., Colton, M. and Williams, M. (1997) *International Perspectives on Family Support.* Aldershot, Ashgate Publishing.

Hennessey, E. (1999) Children as Service Evaluators. *Child Psychology and Psychiatry Review.* 4: 4, 153–161.

Hester, M., Pearson, C. and Harwin, N. (2000) *Making an Impact: Children and Domestic Violence.* Jessica Kingsley, London.

Hetherington, D. and Baistow, S. (2001) Supporting Families with a Mentally Ill Parent: European Perspectives on Interagency Cooperation. *Child Abuse Review*, 10: 351–365.

Hill, J., Fonagy, P., Safier, E. and Sargent, J. (2003) The Ecology of Attachment in the Family: The Theoretical Basis for the Development of a Measure. *Family Process.*

Hill, M. (1999) *Effective Ways of Working with Children and their Families.* London, Jessica Kingsley.

Hill, M., Laybourn, A. and Borland, M. (1996) Engaging with Primary-aged Children about their Emotions and Wellbeing: Methodological Considerations. *Children and Society,* 10: 129–144.

Hodes, M. (1998) Refugee Children May Need a Lot of Psychiatric Help. *British Medical Journal*, 316, 793–4.

Hoffman, L. (1981) *Foundations of Family Therapy.* New York, Basic Books.

Hoffman, L. (1993) *Exchanging Voices: a Collaborative Approach to Family Therapy.* London, Karnac.

Holt, C. (1998) Working with Fathers of Children in Need. In. Bayley R. (Ed.) *Transforming Children's Lives: the Importance of Early Intervention.* London, Family Policy Studies Centre.

Holterman, S. (1995) *All our Futures: The Impact of Public Expenditure and Fiscal Policies on Britain's Children and Young People.* Barkingside, Barnardos.

Home Office (1997) *Social Trends.* London, HMSO.

Home Office (2000) *Living without Fear: Multi-agency Guidance for Addressing Domestic Violence.* London, HMSO.

Home Office (2000) *Race Relations (Amendment) Act.* London, HMSO.

Home Office (2002) *The Nationality, Immigration and Asylum Bill.* London, HMSO.

House of Commons (1997) *Health Committee Report into Child and Adolescent Mental Health Services.* London, HMSO.

Howe, D. (1989) *The Consumers' View of Family Therapy.* London, Gower.

Howe, D., Brandon, M., Hinings, D. and Schofield, G. (1999) *Attachment Theory, Child Maltreatment and Family Support.* Basingstoke, Macmillan.

Issit, M. (1995) Competence, Professionalism and Equal Opportunities. In: Hodgkinson, P. and Issit, M. (Eds.) *The Challenge of Competence.* London, Cassell.

Iwaniec, D. (1995) *The Emotionally Abused and Neglected Child: Identification, Assessment and Intervention.* Chichester, Wiley.

JCWI (2002) *Response to the White Paper, Secure Borders Safe Havens: Integration with Diversity.* London, JCWI.

Johnson, S.M. and Best, M. (2003) A Systemic Approach to Restructuring Adult Attachment. The EFT Model of Couple's Therapy. In: Erdman, P. and Caffery, T. *Attachment and Family Systems.* New York and Hove: Brunner Routledge.

Johnson, S.M. and Makinen, J.A. and Millikin, J.W. (2001) Attachment Injuries in Couple Relationships: A New Perspective on Impasse in Couples Therapy. *Journal of Marital and Family Therapy,* 27: 2, 145–155.

Jones, C. (1997) Poverty. In: Davies, M. (Ed.) *The Blackwell Companion to Social Work.* Oxford, Blackwell.

Josse, J., James, J. and Roland, J. (2003) Diabetes Control in Pregnancy: Who Takes Responsibility for What? *Practical Diabetes International*, 20: 8, 290–293.

Kalnins, I., McQueen, D., Backett, K., Curtice, L. and Currie, C. (1992) Children Empowerment and Health Promotion: Some New Directions in Research and Practice. *Health Promotion International*. 7: 1, 53–59.

Kashani, J. and Allan, W. (1998) *The Impact of Family Violence on Children and Adolescents*. London, Sage.

Kay-Shuttleworth, J. (1832) *The Moral and Physical Condition of the Working Classes Employed in the Cotton Manufacture in Manchester*. Ridgway. (1987) reprint Burney, E.L. (Ed.) Liverpool, Acorn Press.

Keitner, G.I., Ryan, C.E., Fodor, J., Miller, I.W., Epstein, N.B., Bishop, D.S. (1990) A Cross-cultural Study of Family Functioning. *Contemporary Family Therapy,* 12: 5, 439–454.

Keitner, G.I., Ryan, C.E., Miller, I.W. and Norman, W.H. (1992) Recovery and Major Depression: Factors Associated with Twelve-month Outcome. *American Journal of Psychiatry*, 149: 1, 93–99.

Kelly, L. (1996) When Woman Protection is the Best Kind of Child Protection: Children, Domestic Violence and Child Abuse, *Administration*, 44: 2, 118–135.

Kelsall, J. and McCullough, B. (1988) *Family Work in Residential Child Care*. Manchester, Boys and Girls Welfare Society.

Kelson, M. (1995) *Consumer Involvement Initiatives in Clinical Audit and Outcomes*. London, College of Health.

Kemps, C. (1997) Approaches to Working with Ethnicity and Cultural issues. In: Dwivedi. K. (Ed.) *Enhancing Parenting Skills*. London, Wiley.

Kenny, D.A. and LaVoie, L. (1984) The Social Relations Model. In: Berkowitz, L. (Ed.) *Advances in Experimental Social Psychology*. Orlando, Fl, Academic Press.

Kent, H. and Read, J. (1998) Measuring Consumer Participation in Mental Health Services: Are Attitudes Related to Professional Orientation? *International Journal of Social Psychiatry*. 44: 4, 295–310.

Kerridge, L., Lowe, M. and Henry, D. (1998) Ethics and Evidence Based Medicine. *British Medical Journal*, 316: 1151–1153.

Kiddle, C. (1999) *Traveller Children: a Voice for Themselves*. London, Jessica Kingsley.

Kim, W.J. (1995) A Training Guideline of Cultural Competence for Child and Adolescent Psychiatric Residencies. *Child Psychiatry and Human Development*. 26: 2, 125–36.

Kitzinger, J. (1994) The Methodology of Focus Groups: the Importance of Interaction between Research Participants. *Sociology of Health and Fitness*. 16: 1, 103–120.

Kozlowska, K. and Hanney, L. (2002) The Network Perspective: An Integration of Attachment and Family Systems Theories. *Family Process*, 43: 3, 285–312.

Kurtz, Z. (1996) *Treating Children Well: a Guide to Using the Evidence base in Commissioning and Managing Services for the Mental Health of Children and Young People*. London, Mental Health Foundation.

Kurtz, Z. (2001) *Report on Evaluation of CAMHS Innovation Projects*. (unpublished). London, Young Minds.

Kurtz, Z., Thornes, R. and Wolkind, S. (1994) *Services for the Mental Health of Children and Young People in England*. London, Maudsley Hospital.

Lader, D., Singleton, N. and Meltzer, H. (1997) *Psychiatric Morbidity Among Young Offenders in England and Wales*. London, HMSO.

Laing, R.D. (1969) *Interventions in Social Situations*. London, Philadelphia Association.

Lansdowne, G. (1995) *Taking Part: Children's Participation in Decision-making*. London, IPPR.

Larner, G. (2000) Towards a Common Ground in Psychoanalysis and Family Therapy: on Knowing Not to Know. *Journal of Family Therapy*, 22: 61–82.

Lask, B. (1979) Family Therapy Outcome Research. *Journal of Family Therapy,* 14: 2, 87–91.

Lau, A. (1988) Family Therapy and Ethnic Minorities. In: Street, E. and Dryden, W. (Eds.) *Family Therapy in Britain*. Milton Keynes, Open University Press.

Lau, A. (1995) Ethnocultural and religious issues. In: Burck, C. and Speed, B. (Eds.) *Gender Power and Relationships*. London, Routledge.

Leathard, A. (1994) *Going Inter-professional*. London. Routledge.

Leighton, A.H. (1981) Culture and Psychiatry. *Canadian Journal of Psychiatry*, 26: 8, 522–529.

Leonard, P. (1997) *Postmodern Welfare: Reconstructing an Emancipatory Project*. London, Sage.

Leslie, L. and Morton, G. (2001) Family Therapy's response to Family Diversity. *Journal of Family Issues,* 22: 7, 904–921.

Levine, H. (1993) Context and Scaffolding in Developmental Studies of Mother–child Problem-solving Dyads. In: Chaiklin, S. and Lave, J. (Eds.) *Understanding Practice*. Cambridge, Cambridge University Press.

Little, M. and Mount, K. (1999) *Prevention and Early Intervention with Children in Need*. Aldershot, Ashgate.

Llewelyn, S. (1988) Psychological Therapy as Viewed by Clients and Therapists. *British Journal of Clinical Psychology*. 27: 223–237.

Lloyd, E. (Ed.) (1999) *Parenting Matters: What Works in Parenting Education?* London, Barnardos.

Long, J. (1996) Working with Lesbians, Gays and Bisexuals: Addressing Heterosexism in Supervision. *Family Process*, 35: 377–388.

Macdonald, G. (1999) Social Work and Its Evaluation: A Methodological Dilemma? In Williams, F., Popay, J. and Oakley, A. *Welfare Research: A Critical Review*. London, UCL Press.

Macdonald, G. and Roberts, H. (1995) *What Works in the Early Years? Effective Interventions for Children and their Families*. Barkingside, Barnardos.

MacFarlane, A. and McPherson, A. (1995) Primary Healthcare and Adolescence. *British Medical Journal*. 311: 825–826.

Madanes, C. (1981) *Strategic Family Therapy*. San Francisco, Jossey-Bass.

Magrab, P., Evans, P. and Hurrell, P. (1997) Integrated Services for Children and Youth at Risk: an International Study of Multi-disciplinary Training. *Journal of Interprofessional Care*. 11: 1, 99–108.

Main, M. and Goldwyn, R. (1991) Interview-based Adult Attachment Classification: Related to Marvin, R.S. and Stewart, R.B. (1990) A Family Systems Framework for the Study of Attachment. In: Greenberg, M.T., Cicchetti, D. and Cummings, E.M. *Attachment in the Pre-school Years*. University of Chicago Press.

Main, M., Kaplan, N. and Cassidy, J. (1985) Security in Infancy, Childhood and Adulthood: A Move to the Level of Representations. *Monographs of the Society for Research in Child Development*, 50: 1–2, 66–104.

Manor, O. (1991) Assessing the Work of a Family Centre, *Journal of Family Therapy,* 13: 285–294.

Marshal, M., Feldman, R. and Sigal, J. (1989) The Unravelling of a Treatment Paradigm: a Follow-up Study of the Milan approach to family therapy. *Family Process,* 28: 457–470.

Martin, G., Rozanes, P., Pearce, C. and Alison, S. (1995) Adolescent Suicide, Depression and Family Dysfunction. *Acta Psychiatrica Scandinavica*. 92: 336–344.

Marvin, R.S. and Stewart, R.B. (1990) A Family Systems Framework for the Study of Attachment. In: Greenberg, M.T., Cicchetti, D. and Cummings, E.M. *Attachment in the Pre-school Years*. Chicago, Ill, University of Chicago Press.

Mas, C., Alexander, J. and Barton, C. (1985) Modes of Expression in Family Therapy: a Process Study of Roles and Gender. *Journal of Family and Marital Therapy*. 11: 411–415.

Mayall, B. (1994) *Children's Childhoods Observed and Experienced*. Lewes, England.

Mayer and Timms (1970) *The Client Speaks: Working Class Impressions of Casework*. Routledge & Kegan Paul.

McGlone, F., Park, A. and Smith, K. (1998) *Families and Kinship*. London, Family Policy Studies Centre.

McGoldrick, M. and Carter, E.A. (1980) *The Family Life Cycle: A Framework for Family Therapy*. Gardner Press, Inc. New York.

McGoldrick, M., Pearce, J. and Giordano, J. (Eds.) (1982) *Ethnicity and Family Therapy*. New York, Guilford Press.

McGurk, H. (Ed.) (1992) *Childhood and Social Development*. London, Lawrence Earlbaum.

Mental Health Foundation (1999) *The Big Picture*. London, Mental Health Foundation.

Mental Health Foundation (2002) *The Mental Health Needs of Young Offenders*. London, Mental Health Foundation.

Messent, P. (1992) Working with Bangladeshi Families in the East End of London. *Journal of Family Therapy*. 14: 3, 287–305.

Micklewright, J. and Stewart, K. (2000) *Well-being of Children in the European Union, New Economy*. London, Institute for Public Policy Research.

Middleton, L. (1997) *The Art of Assessment*. Birmingham, Venture Press.

Mikulincer, M. and Florian, V. (1999) The Association Between Parental Reports of Attachment Style and Family Dynamics, and Offspring's Report of Adult Attachment Style. *Family Process*, 38: 2, 243–257.

Mikulincer, M., Florian, V., Cowan, P.A. and Cowan, C.P. (2002) Attachment Security in Couple Relationships: A Systemic Model and its Implications for Family Dynamics. *Family Process*, 43: 3, 405–434.

Miller, G. and Prinz, R. (1990) Enhancement of Social Learning Family Interventions for Childhood Conduct Disorders. *Psychological Bulletin*. 108: 291–307.

Miller, I.W., Ryan, C.E., Keitner, G.I., Bishop, D.S. and Epstein, N.B. (2000) The McMaster Approach to Families: Theory, Assessment, Treatment and Research. *Journal of Family Therapy*, 22: 2, 168–189.

Milner, J, and O'Byrne, P. (1998) *Assessment in Social Work Practice*. London, Macmillan.

Minuchin, S. (1974) *Families and Family Therapy*. London, Tavistock Publications.

Minuchin, S. (1984) *Family Kaleidoscope*. Cambridge and London, Harvard University Press.

Modood, T. and Berthoud, R. (1997) *Ethnic Minorities in Britain*. London, Policy Studies Institute.

Moffic, H. and Kinzie, J. (1996) The History and Future of Cross-Cultural Psychiatric Services. *Community Mental Health Journal*. 32: 6, 581–92.

Morris, J. (1998) *Accessing Human Rights: Disabled Children and the Children Act*. Barkingside, Barnardos.

Morris, K. and Tunnard, J. (1996) *Family Group Conferences: Messages from UK Practice and Research*. London, FRG.

Morrison, T.L., Urquiza, A.J. and Goodlin-Jones, B.L. (1997) Attachment and the Representation of Intimate Relationships in Adulthood. *Journal of Psychology*, 131: 1, 57–71.

Morrow, V. (1998) *Understanding Families: Children's Perspectives*. London, National Children's Bureau.

Morrow, V. and Richards, M. (1996) The Ethics of Social Research with Children: An Overview. *Children and Society*. 10: 90–105.

Mullender, A. and Ward, D. (1991) *Self Directed Groupwork: Users take Action for Empowerment*. London. Whiting and Birch.

Mun, E., Fitzgerald, H., Von Eye, A., Puttler, L. and Zucker, R. (2001) Temperamental Characteristics as Predictors of Externalising and Internalising Child Behaviour Problems in the Contexts of High and Low Parental Psychopathology. *Infant Mental Health Journal*, 22: 3, 393–415.

Muncie, J., Wetherell, M., Dallos, R. and Cochrane, A. (Eds) (1997) *Understanding the Family*. London, Sage.

Munley, A., Powers, C.S. and Williamson, J.B. (1982) Humanising Nursing Home Environments: The Relevance of Hospice Principles. *International Journal of Ageing and Human Development*. 15: 263–284.

NCH Action for Children. (2000) *Fact File*. London, NCH.

Nelson, E. (2003) Ethical Concerns Associated with Childhood Depression. *Bioethics Forum*, 18: 3–4, 55–62.

Newfield, S.A., Newfield, N.A., Sperry, J.A. and Smith, T.E. (2000) Ethical Decision Making Among Family Therapists and Individual Therapists. *Family Process*, 39: 2, 177–188.

NISW/DoH Barclay Report (1982) *Social Workers: Their Role and Task*. London, Bedford Square Press.

Nixon, C. and Northrup, D. (1997) *Evaluating Mental Health Services: How Do Programmes for Children Work in the Real World?* Thousand Oaks, CA, Sage.

Oberhuemer, P. (1998) A European Perspective on Early Years Training. In Abbott, L. and Pugh, G. (Eds.) *Training to Work in the Early Years: Developing the Climbing Frame*. Buckingham, Open University Press.

O'Sullivan, T. (1999) *Decision Making in Social Work*. London, Macmillan.

Office for National Statistics (2001) *Child and Adolescent Mental Health*. London, HMSO.

Office for National Statistics (2002) *Social Tends 32*. London, HMSO.

OFSTED (1996) *Exclusions from Secondary Schools 1995–96*, London, HMSO.

Pierson, J. (2002) *Tackling Social Exclusion*. London, Routledge.

Oliver, M. (1996) *Understanding Disability: from Theory to Practice*. London, Macmillan.

Olsen, D.H., Porter, J. and Lavee, Y. (1985) *Faces III*. St. Paul, MN: Family Social Science, University of Minnesota.

Onyet, S., Heppleston, T. and Bushnell, N. (1994) *A National Survey of Community Mental Health Teams: 1 Team Structure*. Sainsbury Centre for Mental Health, London.

Ovretveit, J. (1996) Five Ways to Describe a Multi-disciplinary Team. *Journal of Interprofessional Care*. 10: 2, 163–171.

Papadopoulos, R. (2001) Refugee Families: Issues of Systemic Supervision. *Journal of Family Therapy*, 23: 405–422.

Parton, N. (1999) Reconfiguring Child Welfare Practices: Risk, Advanced Liberalism and the Government of Freedom. In: Chambon, A.S., Irving, A. and Epstein, L. (Eds.) *Reading Foucault for Social Work*. Chichester, Columbia Press.

Parton, N. and O'Byrne, P. (2000) *Constructive Social Work*. London, Macmillan.

Patmore, C. and Weaver, T. (1991) *Community Mental Health Teams: Lessons for Planners and Managers. Good Practices in Mental Health*. London, Harrow.

Payne, M. (1997) *Modern Social Work Theory*, London, Macmillan.

Pearce, J. B. (1999) Collaboration between the NHS and Social Services in the Provision of Child and Adolescent Mental Health Services: a Personal View. *Child Psychology and Psychiatry Review*. 4: 4, 150–152.

Perelberg, R.J. and Miller, A.C. (1990) *Gender and Power in Families*. London, Routledge.

Phillipson, J. (1993) *Practising Equality: Women, Men and Social Work*. London, CCETSW.

Pinkerton, J., Higgins, K. and Devine, P. (2000) *Family Support: Linking Project Evaluation to Policy Analysis*. Aldershot, Ashgate.

Platt, D. and Edwards, A. (1996) Planning a Comprehensive Family Assessment. *Practice*. 9: 2.

Pocock, D. (1997) Feeling Understood in Family Therapy, *Journal of Family Therapy*, 19: 283–302.

Pollard, A. (1987) Studying Children's Perspectives: a Collaborative Approach. In: Walford, G. (Ed.) *Doing Sociology of Education*. Lewes, England Falmer Press.

Powell, J. and Lovelock, R. (1992) *Changing Patterns of Mental Health Care*. London, Avebury.

Preli, R. and Bernard, J.M. (1993) Making Multi-culturalism Relevant for Majority Culture Graduate Students. *Journal of Marital and Family Therapy*, 19: 1, 5–17.

Priestly, M. (1999) *Disability Politics and Community Care*. London, Jessica Kingsley.

Priestly, M. (2001) *Disability and the Life Course: Global Perspectives*. Cambridge, Cambridge Univerity Press.

Pugh, G. and Smith, C. (1996) *Learning to be a Parent*. London, Family Policy Studies Centre.

Ramon, S. (1999) Social Work. In: Bhui, K. and Olajide, D. (Eds.) *Mental Health Service Provision for a Multi-cultural Society*. London, Saunders.

Rank, M.R. (2000) Socialisation of Socio-economic Status. In: Nichols, W.C., Pace-Nichols, M.A., Becvar, D.S. and Napier, A.Y. (Eds.) *Handbook of Family Development and Intervention*. New York, Wiley.

Rawlinson, S. and Williams, R. (2000) The Primary/secondary Care Interface in Child and Adolescent Mental Health Services: the Relevance of Burden. *Current Opinion in Psychiatry*. 13: 389–395.

Rawson, D. (1994) Models of Interprofessional Work: Likely Theories and Possibilities. In: Leathard, A. (Ed.) *Going Interprofessional: Working Together for Health and Welfare*. London, Routledge.

Read, J. and Barker, S. (1996) *Not just Sticks and Stones. A Survey of the Stigma, Taboo and Discrimination Experienced by People with Mental Health Problems*. London, MIND.

Reimers, A.S. and Treacher, A. (1995) *Introducing User-friendly Family Therapy*. London, Routledge.

Remschmidt, H. (Ed.) (2001) *Schizophrenia in Children and Adolescents*. Cambridge, Cambridge University Press.

Repper, J., Saycem L.l., Strong, S., Wilmot, J. and Haines, M. (1997) *Tall Stories from the Back Yard*. London, MIND.

Richardson, J. and Joughin, C. (2000) *The Mental Health Needs of Looked After Children*. Gaskell, London.

Rivett, M. and Street, E. (2003) *Family Therapy in Focus*. Sage Publications, London.

Robbins, D. (1998) The Refocusing Children's Initiative: an Overview of Practice. In: Bayley, R. (Ed.) *Transforming Children's Lives: the Importance of Early Intervention*. London, Family Policy Studies Centre.

Rodney, C. (2000) Pathways: A Model Service Delivery System. In: Singh, N., Leung, J.P. and Singh, A. (2000) *International Perspectives on Child and Adolescent Mental Health*. London, Elsevier.

Rogers, A., Pilgrim, D. and Lacey, R. (1993) *Experiencing Psychiatry: Users Views of Services*.

Rossi, P. (1992) Assessing Family Preservation Programmes. *Children and Youth Services Review*, 14: 77–97.

Roth, A. and Fonagy, P. (1996) *What Works for Whom? A Critical Review of Psychotherapy Research*. London, Guilford Press.

Royal College of Psychiatrists (2002) *Parent-training Programmes for the Management of Young Children with Conduct Disorders. Findings from Research*, London, RCP.

Rutter, M. (1985) Resilience in the Face of Adversity. *British Journal of Psychiatry*. 147: 598–611.

Rutter, M. (1995) *Psychosocial Disturbances in Young People: Challenges for Prevention*. Cambridge, Cambridge University Press.

Rutter, M. and Smith, D. (1995) *Psychosocial Disorders in Young People*. London, Wiley.

Rutter, M., Hersov, L. and Taylor, E. (1994) *Child and Adolescent Psychiatry*. Oxford, Blackwell Scientific.

Ryan, C. (2002) Safeguards for Research Subjects: Who's Watching Whom? *Behavioural Healthcare Tomorrow, June*, 9–11.

Salmon, D. and Hall, C. (1999) Working with Lesbian Mothers: their Healthcare Experiences. *Community Practitioner*. 72: 12, 396–397.

Sandbaek, M. (1999) Children with Problems: Focusing on Everyday Life. *Children and Society*. 13: 106–118.

Save the Children (2001) *Denied a Future? The Right to Education of Roma/Gypsy Traveller Children in Europe*. London, Save the Children.

Scott, R.L. and Cordova, J.V. (2002) The Influence of Adult Attachment Styles on the Association between Marital Adjustment and Depressive Symptoms. *Journal of Family Psychology*, 16: 2, 199–208.

Sebuliba, D. and Vostanis, P. (2001) Child and Adolescent Mental Health Training for Primary Care Staff. *Clinical Child Psychology and Psychiatry*. 6: 2, 191–204.

Shadish, W.R., Ragsdale, K., Glaser, R.R. and Montgomery, L.M. (1995) The Efficacy and Effectiveness of Marital and Family Therapy: A Perspective from Meta-analysis. *Journal of Marital and Family Therapy*, 21: 345–360.

Shapiro, J.P., Welker, C.J. and Jacobson, B.J. (1997) The Youth Client Satisfaction Questionnaire: Development, Construct, Validation, and Factor Structure. *Journal of Child Clinical Psychology*. 26: 87–98.

Shardlow, S. and Payne, M. (1998) *Contemporary Issues in Social Work: Western Europe*. Aldershot, Arena.

Sharkey, P. (2000) *The Essentials of Community Care: A Guide for Practitioners*. London, Macmillan.

Sharpsteen, D.J. and Kirkpatrick, L.A. (1997) Romantic Jealousy and Adult Romantic Attachment. *Journal of Personal and Social Psychology*, 72: 3, 627–640.

Sheldon, B. and Chilvers, R. (2000) *Evidence-based Social Care*. Lyme Regis, Russell House Publishing.

Simonian, S.J., Tarowski, K., Park, A. and Bekney, P. (1993) Child, Parent, and Physician Perceived Satisfaction with Pediatric Outpatient Visits. *Developmental and Behavioural Paediatrics*. 14: 8–12.

Singh, N., Leung, J. and Singh, A. (2000) *International Perspectives on Child and Adolescent Mental Health*. Oxford, Elsevier.

Smale, G., Tuson, G. and Statham, D. (2000) *Social Work and Social Problems*. Basingstoke, Palgrave.

Smith, S., Rosen, K., McCollum, E., Coleman, J. and Herman, S. (1996). The Voices of Children: Pre-adolescent Children's Experiences in Family Therapy. *Journal of Marital and Family Therapy*. 22: 69–86.

Snelgrove, S. and Hughes, D. (2000) Interprofessional Relations Between Doctors and Nurses. Perspectives from South Wales. *Journal of Advanced Nursing*. 31: 3, 661–667.

Social Exclusion Unit (2002) *Reducing Re-Offending by ex-Offenders*, London, HMSO.

Social Services Inspectorate. (1998) *Partners in Planning: Approaches to Planning Services for Children and their Families*. London. HMSO.

Speak, S., Cameron, S., Woods, R. and Gilroy, R. (1995) *Young Single Mothers: Barriers to Independent Living*. London, Family Policy Studies Centre.

Stahmann, R. (2000) Premarital Counselling: a Focus for Family Therapy. *Journal of Family Therapy*. 22: 104–116.

Stanton, M. and Shadish, W. (1997) Outcome, Attrition and Family-couples Treatment for Drug Abuse: a Meta-analysis and Review of the Controlled Comparative Studies. *Psychological Bulletin*. 122: 170–191.

Statham, J. (2000) *Outcomes and Effectiveness of Family Support Services: A Research Review*. London, Institute of Education.

Stephens, J. (2002) *The Mental Health Needs of Homeless Young People*. London, Mental Health Foundation.

Strickland Clark, L., Campbell, D. and Dallos, R. (2000) Children's and Adolescent's Views on Family Therapy. *Journal of Family Therapy*. 22: 324–341.

Stuntzer-Gibson, D., Koren, P. and DeChillo, N. (1995) The Youth Satisfaction Questionnaire: What Kids Think of Services. *Families in Society*. 76: 616–624.

Sue, D., Ivey, A. and Penderson, P. (1996) *A Theory of Multi-cultural Counselling and Therapy*. Brooks/Cole Publishing.

Sutton, C. (1999) *Helping Families with Troubled Children*. Chichester, Wiley.

Sveaass, N. and Reichelt, S. (2001) Refugee Families in Therapy: from Referrals to Therapeutic Conversations. *Journal of Family Therapy*, 23: 119–135.

Sylva, K. (1994) School Influences on Children's Development. *Journal of Child Psychology and Psychiatry and Allied Professions*. 35: 1, 135–170.

Taylor, B. and Devine, D. (1993) *Assessing Needs and Planning Care in Social Work*. London, Arena.

Taylor, C. and White, S. (2000) *Practising Reflexivity in Health and Welfare*. Buckingham, Open University Press.

Thoburn, J., Wilding, J, and Watson, J. (1998) *Children in Need: A Review of Family Support Work in Three Local Authorities*. Norwich, University of East Anglia/Dept of Health.

Thomas, N. and O'Kane, C. (1998) The Ethics of Participatory Research with Children. *Children and Society*. 12: 82–96.

Thompson, N. (2002) *Building the Future: Social Work With Children, Young People and Their Families*. Lyme Regis, Russell House Publishing.

Tiller, P. (1988) Barn Som sakkyndige informanter (Children as reliable sources of information). In: Jensen, M.K. (Ed.) *Interview Med Born (Interviews with Children)* National Institute of Social Research, Copenhagan.

Toledano, A. (1996) Issues Arising from Intercultural Family Therapy. *Journal of Family Therapy*, 18: 289–301.

Treacher, A. (1995) Reviewing Consumer Studies of Therapy. In: Treacher, A. and Reimers, S. *Introducing User-Friendly Family Therapy*. London, Routledge.

Treacher, A. and Carpenter, J. (Eds.) (1984) *Using Family Therapy*. Oxford, Blackwell.

Treseder, P. (1997) *Empowering Children and Young People: A Training Manual for Promoting Involvement in Decision-making*. London, Save the Children.

Trevino, F. (1999) Quality of Health Care for Ethnic/racial Minority Populations. *Ethnicity and Health*. 4: 3, 153–164.

Trevithick, P. (2000) *Social Work Skills*. Buckingham, Open University Press.

Triseliotis, J. (1995) *Teenagers and the Social Work Services*. London, HMSO.

Tucker, S., Strange, C., Cordeaux, C., Moules, T. and Torrance, N. (1999) Developing an Interdisciplinary Framework for the Education and Training of those Working with Children and Young People. *Journal of Interprofessional Care*. 13: 3, 261–270.

Tunstill, J. (1996) Family Support: Past Present and Future Challenges. *Child and Family Social Work*. 1: 151–158.

United Nations (1989) *Convention on the Rights of the Child*. Geneva, UN.

United Nations (1998) *Human Rights Act*. Geneva, UN.

Utting, D. (1995) *Family and Parenthood: Supporting Families, Preventing Breakdown*. York, Joseph Rowntree Foundation.

Van Den Berg, J. and Grealish, M. (1996) Individualized Services and Supports Through the Wraparound Process: Philosophy and Procedures. *Journal of Child and Family Studies*. 5: 7–21.

Vasta, R., Haith, R. and Miller, S. (1993) *Child Psychology*. John Wiley, New York.

Vincent, J. and Jouriles, E. (Eds.) (2000) *Domestic Violence: Guidelines for Research Informed Practice*. London, Jessica Kingsley.

Von Bertalanffy, L. (1968) *General Systems Theory: Foundation, Development, Application*. New York, Brazillier.

Vostanis, P. and Cumella, S. (1999) *Homeless Children: Problems and Needs*. London. Jessica Kingsley.

Walker, S. (1999) Child Mental Health: Promoting Prevention. *Journal of Child Health Care*. 3: 4, 12–16.

Walker, S. (2001) Domestic Violence: Analysis of a Community Safety Alarm System. *Child Abuse Review*, 10: 170–182.

Walker, S. (2001a) Developing Child and Adolescent Mental Health Services. *Journal of Child Health Care*. 5: 2, 71–76.

Walker, S. (2001b) Consulting with Children and Young People. *The International Journal of Children's Rights*. 9: 45–56.

Walker, S. (2001c) Tracing the Contours of Postmodern Social Work. *British Journal of Social Work*, 31: 29–39.

Walker, S. (2002) Family Support and Social Work Practice: Renaissance or Retrenchment? *European Journal of Social Work*, 5: 1, 43–54.

Walker, S. (2003a) Interprofessional Work in Child and Adolescent Mental Health Services. *Emotional and Behavioural Difficulties*, 8: 3, 189–204.

Walker, S. (2003b) *Social Work and Child and Adolescent Mental Health*. Lyme Regis, Russell House Publishing.

Walker, S. (2003c) Social Work and Child Mental Health-Psycho Social Principles in Community Practice. *British Journal of Social Work*, 33: 673–687.

Walker, S. (2003d) *Working Together for Healthy Young Minds*. Lyme Regis, Russell House Publishing.

Walker, S. and Beckett, C. (2004) *Social Work Assessment and Intervention*. Lyme Regis, Russell House Publishing.

Watkins, D. and Gerong, A. (1997) Culture and Spontaneous Self-concepts among Filipino College Students. *Journal of Social Psychology*. 137: 480–488.

Webb, S. (2001) Some Considerations on the Validity of Evidence-based Practice in Social Work. *British Journal of Social Work*, 31: 57–79.

Webster-Stratton, C. (1997) Treating Children with Early-onset Conduct Problems: a Comparison of Child and Parent Training Interventions. *Journal of Consulting and Clinical Psychology*. 65: 1, 93–109.

White, M. (1995) *Re-authoring lives: Interviews and Essays*. Adelaide, Dulwich Centre Publications.

White, M. and Epston, D. (1990) *Narrative Means to Therapeutic Ends*. New York, Norton.

Whiting, L. (1999) Caring for Children of Differing Cultures. *Journal of Child Health Care*, 3: 4, 33–38.

Williams, B., Catel, I.D., Greenwood, M., LeFevre, S., Murray, I. and Thomas, P. (1999). Exploring Person Centeredness: User Perspectives on a Model of Social Psychiatry. *Health and Social Care in the Community*. 7: 6, 475–482.

Williamson, H. and Butler, I. (1996) No One Ever Listens to Us. In: Cloke, C. and Davies, M. (Eds.) *Participation and Empowerment in Child Protection*. Pitman, London.

Wilson, J. (1999) *Child Focussed Practice*. Karnac Books, London.

Wiseman, B. (1999). Portrait of the Therapist as Shaman. *European Journal of Psychotherapy, Counselling, and Health*. 2: 1, 41–55.

Wolbring, G. (2001) Surviving Eugenics. In: Priestly, M. (Ed.) *Disability and the Life Course.* Cambridge, Cambridge University Press.

Wood, A. (1980) The Origins of Family Work: The Theory and Practice of Family Social Work since 1880. *Australian and New Zealand Journal of Family Therapy*, 17: 1, 19–32.

Young, K. and Haynes, R. (1993) Assessing Population Needs in Primary Health Care: the Problem of GP Attachments. *Journal of Interprofessional Care.* 7: 1, 15–27.

Zavirsek, D. (1995) Social Innovations: a New Paradigm in Central European Social Work: International Perspectives in Social Work v1. University of Ljubljana.